Vegetarian Suppers from Deborah Madison's Kitchen

Also by Deborah Madison
The Greens Cookbook
The Savory Way
Vegetarian Cooking for Everyone
This Can't Be Tofu!
Local Flavors

Vegetarian Suppers
from Deborah Madison's Kitchen

Deborah Madison

broadway books ✳ *new york*

PRINTED IN USA

BROADWAY BOOKS and its logo, a letter B bisected on the diagonal, are trademarks of
Random House, Inc.

Book design by Elizabeth Rendfleisch
Photographs by Laurie Smith

ISBN 0-7679-1627-1

contents

For Doe,
who always puts supper
on her table

ACKNOWLEDGMENTS

For Patrick McFarlin, many kisses and a great big rib eye for considerable patience with supper recipes that didn't always work out the first time and for your evermore honest critiques.

The pictures would not have been made without a wonderful team of talented friends. Thank you all—Laurie Smith for your beautiful photographs and ever-cheerful disposition, the altogether fabulous Marja Martin for taking over on the styling front, Kathi Long for your beautiful knife work, and Kimberly Sweet for your excellent support in the kitchen. Without such a team, there would be no pictures. And without the generous support of Judith Espinar and the Clay Angel staff, we wouldn't have all those pretty dishes in the pictures either.

Greg O'Byrne, friend, neighbor, producer of the Santa Fe Wine and Chile Fiesta, and generous sharer of food and wine, provided the wine notes. Certainly people are as individual about wine pairings as they are about food, but I've always found Greg's wine sensibility a good fit with my food. While I always enjoy his wine choices, he's much better on the specifics than I am, and I am grateful to him for his thoughtful notes and years of experience drinking wine with food.

There are many cooks, writers, and food experts who have in one way or another helped in the creation of the suppers, through the inspiration that has come from their kitchens and their writings—Neelam Batra, Anne Bianchi, Nancy Harmon Jenkins, Evan Kleinman, Greg O'Byrne, Richard Olney, Nathalie Waag, Alice Waters, and Laura Werlin. Thank you all for your inspiration.

And of course there wouldn't be books without the belief and support of a publisher, an editor, and an agent. Thank you, Stephen Rubin and Jennifer Josephy, for the challenge of creating 101-plus vegetarian suppers that are worth their salt. And, as always, my gratitude to Doe Coover for representing me with such passionate conviction.

Finally, I would like to thank my readers who have written, called, and otherwise introduced yourselves to me over the years. I can truly say that these recipes are written for you.

i love supper. It's friendly and relaxed. It's easy to invite people over for supper, for there's a quality of comfort that isn't always there with dinner, a meal that suggests more serious culinary expectations—truly a joy to meet, but not all the time. Supper, on the other hand, is for when friends happen to run into each other at the farmers' market or drop in from out of town. Supper is for Sunday night or a Thursday. Supper can be impromptu, it can be pot luck, and it can break the formality of a classic menu. With supper, there's a willingness to make do with what's available and to cook and eat simply. It can also be special and beautifully crafted if that's what you want.

This collection of supper recipes is, for the most part, for straightforward weeknight and weekend dishes that are made from authentic, seasonal foods with flavors to match. More than just dishes, these are really recipes for *menus*. A far cry from those fifteen-minute meals that taste of the brand of tomato sauce you've used, these recipes some-times look long, consisting as they do of two or three elements—squares of grilled polenta, the greens and beans, and a luxurious little Gorgonzola sauce, for example. It's not unlike having meat with a starch and a vegetable. We don't usually eat just one thing for supper, but a small constellation of foods. As you become familiar with this collec-tion of recipes and the dozen suggestions for making supper good, enjoyable, and alto-gether possible, you'll see that they come together with fair ease.

What's been helpful to me in thinking about suppers is not so much the use of short cuts and prepared foods, although leftovers are certainly a boon, but rethinking what the last meal of the day looks like. I'm happy to sauté some spinach, pile it on a rustic piece of toast, drink a friendly little wine, and call that supper.

Supper can be a sandwich. It can be an omelet, eggs baked over smoky-scented po-tatoes, or tofu simmered in a spicy coconut milk sauce. On a hot summer's night, sup-per might consist of a collection of many little appetizers or grilled vegetables with their sauces. On a chilly winter evening, it might well be macaroni and cheese or plump parcels of stuffed cabbage leaves. Sometimes, for my husband and me, supper might be as simple as a roasted sweet potato and a salad.

I've long wanted to put together a collection of vegetarian supper dishes, because after teaching others and observing my own moments of consternation in the kitchen, I'm convinced that coming up with a vegetarian main dish is a big challenge for people. If you cook vegetarian all the time, it's not so hard, of course, because it's a habit. But if you're a "vegophile" like me—you love vegetables and cook vegetarian most of the time, but you also cook fish, an occasional rib eye, or a roast chicken—it's harder because you have to shift gears and mentally start from scratch each time. Why? Because fish, meat, and fowl are the ingrained answer to the question "What's for supper?" For most of us, it's not quite second nature to answer the question with fennel, potatoes, lentils, or a dish like a vegetable flan.

Speaking of flans, Laura Calder, in her charming book *French Food at Home,* writes, "I place [the vegetable flan] in the category of main dishes because it also makes an interesting, attractive supper for nights when I've had it up to the eyeballs with meat." So here's a clue about where to look for vegetarian main dishes and how to think about supper. Those main dishes are hiding right among the first courses in most cookbooks and restaurant menus. Not only vegetarians are delighted by the tasty, small items that begin so many meals; lots of diners like to put a few of them together and call them dinner. I've learned through years of cooking vegetarian food that, with some tweaking, these firsts and sides can assume center position on a menu. In fact, the recipes in this book not only serve as main dishes but also can be deconstructed to serve well as first courses or as side dishes to a meat entree, and many of them can be paired to make a more complex main dish. This allows for everyone—vegetarian, vegan, carnivore, and omnivore—to eat happily at the same table.

I'm far too fond of good cheeses, smidgens of cream, and barnyard eggs ever to become a vegan, but many dishes without dairy and eggs get made in my kitchen, mainly because they happen to be good dishes. I have eaten in vegan restaurants that produce the most amazing creations without an egg or a speck of milk. It can be done, though it takes some jumping through hoops. But vegan dishes you'll encounter here—or vegan adaptations of given recipes—are just as straightforward and culturally familiar as the rest of the recipes.

In this little book you'll meet up with a few old friends—classics in my kitchen—and lots of new ones. There are fast, informal suppers and others that can truly be used for entertaining. The suggestions for side dishes and desserts are drawn from recipes in *Vegetarian Cooking for Everyone* and my most recent book, *Local Flavors: Cooking and Eating from America's Farmers' Markets.* And best of all, you'll find exciting wine suggestions with each recipe, provided by Greg O'Byrne, producer of Santa Fe's Wine and Chile Fiesta. Greg's life is as steeped in the love of wine as mine is in the love of vegetables, and I've learned a great deal from him about putting the right wines with vegetarian dishes. Greg has generously shared his expertise and advice for pairing wines with my dishes, many of which, as neighbor and friend, he is well familiar with.

I hope that you'll enjoy Greg's wine selections, that you'll find these supper dishes delicious and a pleasure to cook, and that they in turn will find a home in your kitchen.

a dozen ideas for making supper good, enjoyable, and altogether possible

Simplify your menu
1.

It's okay to make a meal out of garlicky sautéed kale and a roasted sweet potato. It's plenty of food, and both vegetables offer great little phytonutrients. No, this isn't a meal that's full of protein, but don't worry about it. That may have come from lunch or breakfast, or it will be there tomorrow. It doesn't need to be there at every meal.

Eat less
2.

It's great to feel light when you go to bed and to wake up hungry for breakfast. Consider serving smaller portions of whatever food you like, made with real, quality ingredients. But if what you want is a huge quantity of something to dig into, make it vegetables. Or *a* vegetable. It takes a lot of vegetables to add up to a lot of calories.

Have breakfast or lunch for supper
3.

Mix it up. A fried egg sandwich, ricotta pancakes, mushrooms over toast, or a handheld sandwich—dishes like these can assume a nontaxing role in the evening. Save the lasagne for another time.

Leftovers can be your best friend and they can save a trip to the store. It's easy to turn leftover lentils or polenta into a supper dish. Ratatouille can be used in at least four different ways, and leftover vegetable stews are usually delicious over toast the next day. Extra crêpes or crêpe batter can make a meal in a jiffy. And that extra portion from last night's supper can be a good lunch for the person working at home as well as the one going to the office.

I love dishes, particularly the folk-art dishes that are featured in the pictures in all my books. I would sooner buy a plate than a sweater. To me dishes are as important as the food that goes on them because of the way they flatter food and delight the eye. Like the foods we cook, they are made by hand. Gorgeous terra-cotta gratin dishes, inexpensive Spanish cazuelas just large enough to hold a single portion of something, ramekins, soup plates with rims—all of these artful shapes provide ways to bring focus and style to what you've made, even if it's just an egg baked on a bed of potatoes.

Whatever you learn how to make well, you can make quickly and without a second thought. We all caught on about pasta. Ragouts are my main dish—I can make them with my eyes closed and without a plan. Gratins or savory pies might be yours. When we know a certain type of dish or two well, cooking becomes much easier and less stressful. It makes our cooking flow with ease.

One good reason for becoming passionate about food is that you'll always have a plan in mind for something you want to cook. You know when you have batter in the fridge for those buckwheat crêpes, a dozen eggs from the farmers' market, some fabulous tomatoes, or maybe a leftover potato skillet pie to brown. Having a river of ingredients moving through your kitchen and ideas to match makes coming up with supper easy and enjoyable.

8. Eat locally and seasonally

As always, I encourage you to eat seasonally and shop from your farmers' market. This is where you'll find the best food there is anywhere, so there's less you have to do to make it taste good. It's good already. And, of course, there are all the other pleasures that come with eating locally—being part of your community, doing something important for yourself and your region, being informed about where your food comes from, and experiencing joy in doing so.

9. Cook with others

It is so much more fun when it's not just you in the kitchen, unless, of course, you want to control it. If you're a parent, teach your kids how to use a knife and become masters at making a vinaigrette or a good salad. I know many young girls who love to make crêpes (it was the first food I learned to cook as well). Why not harness that interest in the service of supper? It's more fun for everyone this way.

10. Relax about weights and measures

Does your tofu weigh 19 ounces rather than 16? Is one can of coconut milk 13.5 ounces and another 16 ounces? Does it matter? It doesn't, not in these informal recipes. Sometimes products vary, especially if you buy them in Asian or Latin markets where weights and measures aren't consistent with what's in supermarkets. My advice is to use what you have regardless of the size—the whole block of tofu, the entire can of coconut milk—and don't worry. It's far more useful to have a leftover cooked dish than a little piece of tofu floating in water or a bit of coconut milk hidden in the back of the refrigerator. You know that they'll just end up getting thrown out.

And when it comes to cooking times, there's no absolute for all of our stoves, pots and pans, flames and heat levels—even altitudes vary. The "low" on my new stove is the equivalent of "medium" on my former one. A heavy cast-iron pan takes longer to heat, but holds its heat longer than a thin aluminum pan. Ultimately it's our eyes and hands and nose that tell us when something should be turned over or to raise or lower the heat.

There's every reason to choose organic foods—for their flavor, for your health, and for the health of the environment. As long as the standards remain in place—and they are unfortunately threatened on a regular basis—the label *organic* means that your food is produced in a beneficial manner and that it's free from pesticides, herbicides, and genetically modified organisms. We already know that pesticides aren't good for us, wildlife, the water supply, or much else, and that GMOs are not without problems. Choosing organic is, for me, choosing health and vitality, and often flavor. The cost is more, but so is the cost of illness. We are fortunate that today there are organic options available for all kinds of foods.

11. When possible, choose organic foods

Increasingly, we have the opportunity to buy foods that are imbued with the mark of a person's skill and passion. Craft is evident in farmstead cheeses, hearth breads, beautifully grown fruits and vegetables, chocolates, and many other foods. When we leave the imprint of our hands on our meals, we also become craftsmen. Even in preparing supper, we can make something that's our own and no one else's. It is a gift to our families and friends to do this, something to take pride and joy in doing.

12. Become an artisan in your kitchen

The last thing is this: If you want to make the side dishes that have been suggested with each recipe, you can find them in my books *Vegetarian Cooking for Everyone* and *Local Flavors: Cooking and Eating from America's Farmers' Markets*. When it comes to supper, there's no need to reinvent the wheel, after all. Familiarity is a delight.

13. The baker's dozen

*savory pies
and gratins*

*i*f I added up all the savory pies and gratins I've made in my life, they'd comprise a book in themselves. There's an instant appeal and sense of ease about both of these dishes. In my experience, everyone likes pie no matter what's in the crust. As for fragrant gratins, bubbling under their "crust" of bread crumbs, they are simply irresistible.

A crust makes a pie a more formal and special dish, but if you're not at ease whipping one out—it really is very easy with some practice—know that I've used the word *pie* very loosely. Some crusts are bread crumbs patted into the dish, and others don't have a crust at all. For the Feta and Ricotta Cheese Pie, it's the rim of the black cast-iron skillet, rather than pie dough, that frames the ingredients. But when you do make the dough given on page 8, note that it is made with less fat than most and with a mixture of whole wheat pastry and all-purpose flour, making it a little crisper and a lot tastier than the usual all-butter white-flour crust.

To make gratins or these shallow pies or tarts a main supper dish, plan to serve a big wedge or a quarter of a 9-inch pie. I like both pies and gratins served with a salad or sautéed greens right on the same plate and a separate vegetable course or soup to start. Serve rich gratins with lighter foods such as crudités for appetizers, thin soups for starters, and the aforementioned greens. In the case of nonstarchy gratins, such as the eggplant gratins on page 12, rice, quinoa, and other grains just drink up their good juices.

Tart Shell

A lower-fat version of the usual buttery crust, this tart shell is a bit crisper than the traditional one. Whole wheat pastry flour gives the dough more substance and flavor than white flour.

$\frac{1}{2}$ **cup whole wheat pastry flour**

$\frac{1}{2}$ **cup plus 2 tablespoons all-purpose flour**

$\frac{3}{8}$ **teaspoon sea salt**

5 tablespoons cold butter, cut into chunks

3 tablespoons sour cream, reduced-fat if you like

ice water

1. Combine the flours and salt in a food processor.

2. Add the butter and pulse to form coarse crumbs, then add the sour cream and pulse again. Dribble in just enough ice water, about 1 tablespoon, to make damp-looking crumbs, working as briefly as possible. Turn the dough out onto a board, gather into a ball, then shape into a disk. Refrigerate for 15 to 30 minutes.

3. Roll the chilled dough into a 10-inch circle, drape it over the rolling pin, then lay it over the tart pan. Gently settle the dough into the pan. Using your fingertips, press the dough against the sides so that they are about $\frac{1}{4}$ inch thick. Freeze for at least 15 minutes or until ready to prebake. Formed tart shells, well wrapped in foil, can be frozen for a week before using.

to prebake   Preheat the oven to 425°F. Place the frozen tart shell on a sheet pan and bake in the center of the oven until lightly colored and set, about 20 minutes. Check a few times during the baking and prick any swollen spots with the sharp tip of a knife.

Onion and Rosemary Tart
with fromage blanc

Fromage blanc is nonfat cheese similar in texture to sour cream and crème fraîche. It lacks the unctuousness of its full-fat cousins, but when baked it's perfectly creamy and smooth.

I like this tart with a robust vegetable, such as roasted artichokes or mushrooms sautéed with spinach and seasoned with lots of pepper. For wine, a bistro-style red such as a Cabernet Franc from France's Loire Valley goes nicely with these straightforward flavors.

Unless you have a tart shell ready, begin by cooking the onions, then make, press, and freeze the shell while they're cooking. Once you've prebaked the tart shell, reduce the oven heat, fill the shell, and put it in the oven about 45 minutes before you're ready to eat. This tart is best eaten warm.

2 teaspoons butter or olive oil	2 teaspoons finely chopped rosemary
4 small or 3 medium onions, quartered and thinly sliced crosswise, at least 4 cups	1 9-inch tart shell (page 8)
	2 eggs
sea salt and freshly ground pepper	1 cup fromage blanc

1. Preheat the oven to 425°F. Melt the butter in a Dutch oven and add the onions. Season with ½ teaspoon salt, give a stir, cover the pan, and cook slowly until soft and pale gold, about 30 minutes. Add the rosemary, then season with pepper and taste, adding more salt if needed.

2. While the onions are cooking, prepare and prebake the tart shell. Then reduce the heat to 350°F.

3. Whisk the eggs with the fromage blanc, ⅜ teaspoon salt, and a little pepper. Stir in the onions, then pour the mixture into the shell. Bake until golden and nearly firm, about 35 minutes. Let rest for 5 minutes, then remove it from the tart pan, set it on a platter, and serve.

Variation with scallions

Scallions take far less time to cook than onions and make a more delicate tart, one that's just right for spring. You'll want 4 bunches of scallions, including a few inches of their greens, thinly sliced. Cook them in the butter until softened, 4 to 5 minutes. Use a spring herb in this version—chervil, tarragon, the first few basil leaves—and serve the tart with asparagus, the first peas, or leeks simmered in wine.

savory pies and gratins

Dried Porcini
and fresh mushroom tart

This succulent mix of mushrooms may tempt you to forget the pastry and just spoon them over some toast—an excellent idea, in fact. But if you want a dish that has more style, make a tart. It will look glorious, and with the full ounce of dried mushrooms it will be intensely mushroomy.

While rich in flavor, this is not a heavy dish, so go ahead and include a soup (a roasted red pepper soup would make a lively start), a side dish (think of roasted carrots with garlic and thyme or braised black kale), and a sprightly green salad. A glass of Bandol rosé is the perfect wine.

Turn on the oven, get the dried mushrooms soaking, then use that window of time to prepare the tart shell (unless you have one ready). and slice the onion and mushrooms. Bake the tart shell while the mushrooms are cooking. This tart can be served hot, warm, or at room temperature.

Note: If you're using portobellos, remove the gills with a spoon before cooking, or the dish will be very dark.

1 ounce (1 cup) dried porcini mushrooms

½ cup dry white wine or dry sherry

1 9-inch tart shell (page 8)

1 tablespoon olive oil or a mixture of butter and oil, plus a little oil to finish

1 large white onion, finely diced

½ pound white or brown mushrooms, sliced ¼ inch thick or less

½ pound (3 small) portobello or other large mushrooms, sliced ¼ inch thick (see note)

sea salt and freshly ground pepper

1 heaping teaspoon tomato paste

1 parsley sprig and a few thyme or marjoram sprigs, minced

1 egg

⅔ cup half-and-half, cream, or Mushroom Stock (page 209)

1. Preheat the oven to 425°F. Put the porcini in a saucepan with the wine and ½ cup water. Bring to a boil, then turn off the heat, cover, and set aside for 30 minutes. Once the porcini are tender, pour the liquid through a fine strainer into a bowl, then chop the mushrooms into ½-inch or smaller pieces. Reserve the soaking water.

2. Meanwhile, prepare and freeze the tart shell.

3. Heat the oil in a wide skillet. Add the onion and cook over medium-high heat, stirring frequently, until it starts to color, about 5 minutes.

4. Add the fresh mushrooms. Raise the heat to high, season with 1 teaspoon salt, and cook, tossing occasionally, until they start to color, about 10 minutes. Stir in the tomato paste and a few tablespoons of the mushroom-soaking liquid, then add the porcini and continue cooking, adding more mushroom liquid in small amounts, until the mush-

rooms are tender and glazed, about 15 minutes. Add half the herbs, then taste for salt and season with pepper.

5. While the mushrooms are cooking, prebake the tart shell.

6. Beat the egg with the half-and-half. Slide the mushrooms into the prebaked tart shell and pour the custard over. Bake until the custard is set, 25 to 30 minutes. When done, sprinkle the remaining herbs over the top and dab a few drops of oil on the mushrooms to make them shine.

SERVES 4

Two Eggplant Tarts
with tomatoes, olives, and goat cheese

In both versions the eggplant can be prepared (roasted or broiled), the custards whisked together, and the tart shells prebaked hours before completing the tarts.

These two tarts use the same ingredients, but with very different effect. In the first, roasted eggplant is beaten into the custard, over which the tomatoes form a pretty coverlet. In the second, the eggplant is sliced and broiled, then mixed with the tomatoes, making a more rustic tart. Both are good to keep in mind when an assortment of tomatoes, such as Sun Gold, Yellow Pear, and Sweet 100, are available—they look and taste gorgeous—and both versions make a fine dinner on a hot night.

I might start this meal with a zucchini and basil soup, include a salad on the plate, and end with a platter of fresh figs and raspberries, possibly accompanied by a Muscat sabayon. A Rhône-style rosé from California's south-central coast, such as an Ojai Vin Gris, would be good with all the elements in these tarts.

Smooth Roasted Eggplant and Tomato Tart

Ideally, you might roast the eggplant over the coals the night before if you're grilling, which adds a rich smoky flavor. Once roasted, the eggplant can wait for several days.

1 9-inch tart shell (page 8)

2 medium eggplants, about 1 pound each

sea salt and freshly ground pepper

1 heaping tablespoon finely slivered basil leaves, plus a few leaves for garnish

2 heaping tablespoons pitted Niçoise olives, finely chopped

1 egg

$^1/_2$ cup half-and-half, cream, or crème fraîche

3 to 4 ounces crumbled goat cheese

2 cups mixed small tomatoes, halved crosswise

olive oil for drizzling

1. Preheat the oven to 425°F. Make and prebake the tart shell. Reduce the heat to 400°F.

2. Pierce the eggplants in several places, then put them on a sheet pan and bake until they're collapsed, about 40 minutes, or roast them over hot coals until collapsed. Set them in a colander for 15 minutes to drain, then scrape the flesh out of the skin, put it in a bowl, and mash coarsely with $^1/_2$ teaspoon salt. Add the basil and olives and season with pepper. Beat the egg with the half-and-half and goat cheese and whisk it into the eggplant.

3. Pour the custard into the tart shell. Cover with tomatoes, cut sides up. Drizzle with olive oil and bake until the custard is set, about 30 minutes. Sliver the reserved basil leaves and scatter them over the hot surface. Let the tart cool for at least 15 minutes or serve at room temperature.

Rustic Eggplant and Tomato Tart

For this tart, use 2 pounds narrow Japanese or Italian eggplants, a few tablespoons olive oil, and an additional $^1/_2$ cup half-and-half.

Make and prebake the tart shell, as in the preceding recipe. Preheat the broiler. Brush a sheet pan lightly with olive oil.

1. Remove strips of the eggplant skin, leaving a few thin bands. Slice diagonally about $^3/_8$ inch thick and toss with 2 to 3 tablespoons olive oil. Place them on the oiled sheet pan in a single layer and broil until golden, 10 to 15 minutes if your broiler is hot. Turn and cook the second side, about 10 minutes. Transfer those that finish first to a bowl. When all are done, season with a few pinches of salt and some pepper.

2. Beat the egg in a small bowl with the half-and-half and goat cheese, leaving the cheese a little chunky.

3. Add the olives, basil, and most of the tomatoes to the eggplant and toss together. Put them in the tart shell and pour the custard over all. Tuck the remaining tomatoes here and there where they can be seen and bake until the custard is set, about 35 minutes. Serve warm or tepid.

Chard and Onion Torta

Both the chard and the onions cook at a gentle pace, so begin with them. This is when you can prep everything else and prepare your baking dish.

This is a slightly more formal variation on that perfumed Provençal frittata, trouchia, one of my favorite dishes. Here the trouchia gets a crust of bread crumbs, which not only spares you the trouble of making a dough but also eliminates $\frac{1}{2}$ cup of butter. To my eyes, this makes it much more acceptable to use light cream for the liquid, which provides a more memorable texture. For chard, I prefer silver-stemmed over red because of the tendency for the red veins to bleed. However, the flavor is fine and if that's what you have, then use it.

You might serve this with sautéed red peppers, simply cooked zucchini, or the chard stems cooked in olive oil. For wine, go with a Provençal rosé or a Spanish rosado from Rioja; or, if you prefer a red, try a lighter-style Côtes-du-Rhône.

2 tablespoons butter or olive oil, plus butter for the dish

2 slices bread, crusts removed, made into crumbs in a food processor

1 large onion, quartered and thinly sliced crosswise

2 pinches of saffron threads

$\frac{1}{4}$ cup slivered basil leaves

1 teaspoon thyme leaves, chopped, or 2 pinches dried

2 big bunches of chard, leaves sliced from the stems and chopped into 1-inch pieces

sea salt and freshly ground pepper

2 garlic cloves, smashed in a mortar with a pinch of salt

1 cup grated Gruyère cheese

$\frac{1}{4}$ cup freshly grated Parmesan cheese, plus a little for the top

3 eggs

1 cup light cream, milk, or Mushroom Stock (page 209)

1. Preheat the oven to 350°F. Generously butter a baking dish, such as a 10-inch round terra-cotta gratin dish, then press the bread crumbs into it, covering the bottom and sides. Reserve any extra crumbs.

2. Heat the 2 tablespoons butter in a nonstick skillet over medium heat. Add the onion, then crumble the saffron threads over it. Cook, stirring frequently, until the onion is very soft, about 15 minutes. If it threatens to burn or crisp, add a little water or white wine to the pan.

3. Add the basil, thyme, and chard to the softened onion and season with $\frac{1}{2}$ teaspoon salt. Cook until the chard has wilted and is tender, stirring occasionally, about 7 minutes. Stir in the garlic, taste for salt, and season with pepper. Transfer the mixture to a bowl and stir in any extra bread crumbs. Add the cheeses, eggs, and cream.

4. Pour the filling into the prepared dish, grate a little extra Parmesan over the top, and bake in the center of the oven until golden and nearly firm throughout, about 30 minutes. Poke a knife tip into the top to make sure the eggs are set. Let rest for several minutes before serving.

Feta and Ricotta Cheese
skillet pie

There's no crust, but you can't argue with this handsome pie, which is rimmed with the black edge of the cast-iron skillet rather than with pastry. It's excellent for those seeking protein-rich dishes, and it's so quick to put together you'll have to wait for your oven to heat up.

Serve this skillet pie in wedges with sides that match the season. In summer, look to roasted peppers plus a few olives; in spring, a shaved fennel salad; in winter, luscious braised black kale. This also makes a good appetizer, served, of course, in smaller portions, or part of a mezze plate (page 162). A lusty Zinfandel from Sonoma would partner well with the cheese.

$^3/_4$ pound feta cheese, preferably sheep's milk

1 pound ricotta cheese

4 to 6 eggs

$^1/_4$ cup flour

$^3/_4$ cup milk

sea salt and freshly ground white pepper

1 tablespoon chopped dill

1. Preheat the oven to 375°F. Mix three-quarters of the feta with the ricotta in a medium bowl, without worrying about getting it perfectly smooth—you'll want some chunks. Beat the eggs into the cheese, then add the flour and milk. Season with $^1/_2$ teaspoon salt, pepper, and dill.

2. Butter a 10-inch cast-iron skillet or an earthenware baking dish. Pour in the batter and crumble the remaining cheese over the top. Bake until golden, 35 to 40 minutes. Cut into wedges and serve with your chosen garnish.

Cabbage and Leek Gratin
with mustard cream

Boil and then drain the cabbage. Whisk the ingredients together for the batter, then combine the two and bake. Just make sure the cabbage is very dry so it doesn't dilute the custard.

This homey gratin is a standard in my kitchen because it's reliably delicious and easy to make. It's also versatile. While it makes no pretensions to grandeur with its rustic good looks, this gratin won't disappoint.

Home-cooked cannellini beans and braised carrots are two great side dishes for this gratin. A Pinot Blanc from Alsace would marry well with the cabbage and the dairy.

$1^{1}/_{2}$ pounds green cabbage, Savoy if possible, chopped into 2-inch squares

3 fat leeks, white parts only, quartered lengthwise, chopped, and washed

sea salt

$^{1}/_{3}$ cup flour

1 cup milk

$^{1}/_{3}$ cup sour cream

3 eggs

3 tablespoons finely chopped parsley or dill

Mustard Cream (recipe follows)

1. Preheat the oven to 350°F and butter or oil a 6-cup gratin dish. Put a large pot of water on to boil for the cabbage. While it's heating, chop the cabbage and the leeks. When the water boils, add salt to taste and the vegetables. After 5 minutes, pour the vegetables into a colander. Press down firmly with a rubber scraper to force out as much water as possible.

2. Whisk the flour, milk, sour cream, eggs, and herbs together, then add the cabbage and leeks. Season with $^{3}/_{4}$ teaspoon salt. Pour into the prepared dish and bake until firm and lightly browned, about 45 minutes. Serve with Mustard Cream.

Mustard Cream

1 small shallot, finely diced

1 teaspoon white wine vinegar

pinch of sea salt

²⁄₃ cup sour cream or whole-milk yogurt

2 to 3 teaspoons prepared mustard, smooth or coarse or mixed with horseradish

Mix the shallot and vinegar in a small bowl with the salt and let stand for 5 minutes. Whisk in the sour cream and mustard. Adjust the seasonings, adding more vinegar or mustard to taste if needed.

some easy variations

- Add shredded, blanched celery root to the gratin.
- Add 2 to 3 ounces grated or crumbled cheese, such as aged Gouda, Gruyère, Reblochon, feta, or a sharp aged Cheddar. Omit the dill with cheeses other than Cheddar.
- Use tarragon with some snipped chives in place of dill.

SERVES 4

Huckleberry Potato
and summer vegetable stovetop "pie"

Assemble and wash your vegetables, get the potatoes cooking, then slice and layer everything else. It takes about 10 minutes to assemble the pie, 30 minutes to cook—without your attention.

vegetarian suppers

It's the way the vegetables are framed in their cast-iron pan that makes the dish a pie, not a crust, which is completely absent. It falls into a ragout the minute it's served, but the initial presentation is gorgeous and the dish is hearty enough that nothing else is needed on the plate. I like to make this dish colorful, starting with the pink-fleshed Huckleberry potatoes (and, when possible, Peruvian All Blues and yellow-fleshed varieties), then building up the layers with yellow and green zucchini, roasted peppers, and finally, orange Sun Gold tomatoes. This dish is vegan.

You might start this vegetable-intense supper with a simple appetizer, such as roasted almonds, baked olives, or lemon cucumbers, and end with a salad and a cool dessert, such as honey ice cream with fresh figs. A ripe vintage Burgundy or New World Pinot Noir from Oregon would both have the bright Pinot fruit and the acidity that this dish needs.

1 pound waxy potatoes, such as Huckleberry, All Blues, or Yellow Finns

3 tablespoons olive oil

3 garlic cloves, thinly sliced

a handful of basil or mint leaves, slightly less of other herbs, coarsely chopped

sea salt and freshly ground pepper

1 large onion, thinly sliced

1 yellow and 1 green zucchini (about ¾ pound), sliced

1 red and 1 yellow bell pepper, roasted and cut into ½-inch strips

16 Sun Gold or other small tomatoes, halved or sliced

1. Scrub, then slice the potatoes into ¼-inch rounds. Heat 1 tablespoon of the oil in a cast-iron skillet over low heat, add the potatoes, stir them about to coat them with the oil, then spread them evenly over the pan. Scatter over a third of the garlic, a third of the herbs, and season with salt and pepper.

2. Add a layer of the onion and zucchini over the potatoes, followed by more garlic and basil, salt and pepper. Add the pepper strips with the remaining garlic and basil, then the tomatoes. Dribble 3 tablespoons water down the sides of the pan and thread the rest of the oil over the top. Raise the heat just enough to get the water bubbling, then cover the pan and reduce the heat to very low.

3. Cook until the vegetables are tender, about 25 minutes, then remove the lid, raise the heat, and reduce the excess liquid by boiling gently for several minutes. Serve warm or at room temperature with Marjoram Pesto (page 175), a basil puree, or homemade mayonnaise. You can even serve this cold as a salad, dressed with capers and a squeeze of lemon.

Crookneck Squash and Rice Gratin
with summer herbs

My friend Nathalie Waag taught me this Provençal dish, which is so comfy and satisfying that I've included other versions of it elsewhere. This is one of those dishes that would make a great side to serve with grilled lamb chops but of course it stands alone as a vegetarian main dish. Thick slices of Beefsteak tomatoes would be excellent on both plates. Without the cheese the dish is vegan.

Come fall and winter, you can make it using grated winter squash and sage and serve braised mustard greens on the side. Serve this summery version with a slightly chilled red from Verona such as Allegrini Valpolicella Classico. A Valpolicella riserva or even an Amarone, both heavier styles made from the same grape (Corvina) in the Veneto, can be served with the winter squash version.

½ cup long-grain rice

sea salt and freshly ground pepper

a good handful of parsley leaves

several bushy marjoram and thyme sprigs

2 garlic cloves

2 tablespoons olive oil, plus extra for the top

2 large leeks, white parts plus a bit of green, quartered lengthwise, chopped, and washed

2 pounds crookneck squash or zucchini, sliced into thin rounds

2 ounces Gruyère cheese, grated (about ½ cup)

1 teaspoon finely grated lemon zest

1. Preheat the oven to 350°F. Lightly oil a 2-quart gratin dish or 4 shallow individual gratin dishes.

2. Bring 1 cup of water to a boil in a small saucepan. Add the rice and a few pinches of salt and simmer until the rice is soft and most of the water is absorbed, about 15 minutes. It's all right if it's a little wet. Set aside.

3. Chop the herbs with the garlic and set aside.

4. Heat 2 teaspoons of the oil in a nonstick skillet over medium-low heat and add the leeks. Cook, stirring frequently, until soft, about 12 minutes. Add a splash of water or dry white wine if necessary to keep them from browning. Season with a few big pinches of the herbs, ½ teaspoon or more salt, to taste, and pepper. Scrape into a bowl, return the pan to the stove, and add 4 teaspoons oil.

5. Raise the heat, add the squash to the skillet, and sauté until golden in places, 4 or 5 minutes. Add about a tablespoon of the herbs and continue to sauté until fairly tender and increasingly colored, a few minutes more. Turn off the heat. Return the leeks to the pan along with the rice and cheese. Toss well, taste for salt, and season with pepper.

6. Set aside 2 tablespoons of the herb mixture and add the rest to the vegetables. Put the vegetables in the prepared dish, drizzle a little oil over the top, and bake until hot throughout, 25 to 30 minutes. Switch the oven to broil and brown the top.

7. Mix the reserved herbs with the lemon zest and toss them over the hot gratin when it comes out of the oven. Serve hot or warm.

Eggplant and Tomato Gratin
three ways

SERVES 4 TO 6
GENEROUSLY

Although I'm always cooking new dishes, this gratin is one I return to every summer. I'm especially fond of it covered with saffron-infused ricotta, à la the late Richard Olney, who influenced so many of today's cooks and whose recipes are justifiably classics. It's also lovely when the eggplant and fresh tomato sauce are simply layered with fresh mozzarella. But it can be made without any dairy at all—just succulent layers of eggplant and tomato with an accent of torn basil leaves.

All of these versions are good served with the saffron rice on page 206, and all are delicious with rosé wines. Or consider an Oregon or Italian Pinot Gris, a lighter-style Italian red, such as a Chianti Classico normale, or even a sparkling red Lambrusco.

These gratins require a good tomato sauce, but that can be made well ahead of time. If you're starting it from scratch, broil the eggplant while it's cooking. You needn't salt the eggplant if it's very fresh, but if less than stellar, salt the slices, let them stand for 30 minutes or more, then rinse and blot them dry before broiling. When the sauce is done, layer the gratin, then bake when ready. Leftovers are delicious reheated in a skillet.

*savory pies
and gratins*

Vegan Eggplant and Tomato Gratin

Fast, Fresh or Long-Cooked Tomato Sauce (page 202 or 203),
    made with at least 2 pounds ripe tomatoes
2½ pounds medium oblong eggplants, Asian or Italian varieties
olive oil
sea salt and freshly ground pepper
several large basil leaves, torn

1. Start the tomato sauce, then preheat the broiler. Lightly oil a 2-quart (or 8- by 10-inch) gratin dish. Once you've got the sauce going, remove bands of the skin from the eggplants with a vegetable peeler, leaving narrow strips of skin attached. Slice the eggplant into ½-inch rounds or ovals. Salt them if you think they need it (see headnote). Lightly brush or spray each slice with olive oil, set on a sheet pan, and broil until golden, about 12 minutes. Broil the second side about 12 minutes, then season lightly with salt and pepper.

2. When the sauce is ready, set the oven at 375°F. Spread a scant third of the tomato sauce in the prepared gratin dish. Make an overlapping layer of half the eggplant and shower it with some of the basil. Add a little more tomato sauce, basil, and the rest of the eggplant. Spoon the remainder of the sauce between the slices of eggplant without covering them completely.

3. Bake until bubbling and hot, about 35 minutes. Let settle for a few minutes before serving.

Eggplant Gratin with Saffron Custard

Make the gratin as described in the preceding recipe, then pour this saffron-ricotta custard over it before baking.

2 eggs

1 cup ricotta cheese

3/4 cup milk

sea salt and freshly ground pepper

2 pinches of saffron threads, soaked in a few tablespoons near-boiling water

1/2 cup finely grated Parmesan cheese

1/2 cup crumbled goat cheese, grated Gruyère, or mozzarella (optional)

Whisk the eggs with the ricotta, milk, and 1/2 teaspoon salt. Stir in the soaked saffron threads followed by the cheeses. Season with pepper. Pour this custard over the gratin and bake until golden and puffed, about 35 minutes.

Eggplant Gratin Layered with Fresh Mozzarella Cheese

The pristine whiteness and molten threads of fresh mozzarella are very appealing, but I'm also attracted to an Italian Fontina here. In fact, there's no reason not to use both. You'll want at least one 4-ounce ball of mozzarella or a scant 1/4 pound thinly sliced Fontina. If using mozzarella, slice it into half-rounds and lay them on paper towels to wick up the water.

To form the gratin, spread the dish with a scant cup of tomato sauce, make a layer of eggplant, then another layer, this time more spare, of tomato sauce. To finish, overlap the remaining eggplant with the cheese and spoonfuls of the remaining tomato sauce so that you have pretty bands of the eggplant, cheese, and tomato. Bake until heated through and bubbling, about 35 minutes.

Potato and Radicchio Gratin

Blanch the radicchio, then start the potatoes. (Parboiling removes strong bitter tones while still leaving it tasting interesting.) While the potatoes are cooking, sauté the onions. Combine all in a gratin dish and bake.

Pot lucks can be a great opportunity for surprising taste buds, and this gratin is inspired by one that showed up at a Slow Food supper in Santa Fe.

If you garden, this recipe will let you harvest your excess radicchio, for three heads won't be too much. Like all greens, their volume diminishes vastly with cooking. But if you don't, and the price of radicchio is high, you can combine it with another green, such as escarole, a relative. Omit the cheese and this becomes vegan.

Serve this substantial gratin with a contrasting vegetable that is neither a starch nor a leaf, such as shredded beets or Delicata squash rings. For wine, a Valpolicella from the Veneto or a Barbera from the Piedmont keeps the geographical ties to the cheese and vegetables close.

sea salt and freshly ground pepper

3 large heads radicchio, or radicchio and escarole, the leaves separated and washed well

1 generous pound yellow-fleshed potatoes, peeled and sliced into ⅓-inch-thick rounds

3 tablespoons olive oil, approximately

1 large onion, thinly sliced

3 ounces Gorgonzola cheese, broken into pieces

1. Preheat the oven to 375°F. Lightly oil an 8- by 10-inch gratin dish. Bring 3 quarts water to a boil in a wide pan and add 1 teaspoon salt. Add the radicchio and simmer for 3 to 5 minutes or until the base of the leaves is tender. Take one out, slice it off, and pop it into your mouth to be sure. Set in a colander to drain.

2. Cover the potatoes with cold water, add salt, then bring to a boil and simmer until tender when pierced with a knife, about 15 minutes. Drain.

3. While the potatoes are cooking, heat 2 teaspoons of the oil in a medium skillet, add the onion, and cook gently until golden and soft, about 8 minutes.

4. Combine the vegetables and toss them gently with a tablespoon of oil. Taste for salt and season with pepper, then settle them into the prepared dish. Poke the cheese into the vegetables and drizzle the rest of the oil over all. Bake until heated through and a bit of crust has formed on the top, about 30 minutes.

Sweet Potato Gratin
with onions and sage

Although my eating habits have improved over the years, I still have a great fondness for creamy gratins, which I make on special occasions. This tender sweet potato gratin is definitely a treat. Don't try to make it with milk—it won't work.

For an accompaniment, look to some authoritative greens, such as a big plate of mustard greens, broccoli rabe, or seared radicchio, or an equally pungent salad of bitter greens. I like something sweet here as well, such as a cranberry relish, apple-quince sauce, or quince compote. For wine, why not go with a creamy rich Chardonnay, such as Martinelli from the Russian River? Cream and butter always go with Chardonnay.

Begin with the onion, and while it's cooking, peel and slice the sweet potatoes. Parboil the potatoes, toss with the onion and seasonings, then pour over the cream and bake.

2 teaspoons oil, plus a little for the dish

1 large onion, chopped into ½-inch dice

2 tablespoons chopped sage or 2 teaspoons dried

3 medium sweet potatoes (about 1½ pounds), thinly sliced

sea salt and freshly ground pepper

a large handful of parsley leaves, chopped with 1 plump garlic clove

¾ cup grated Gruyère or smoked mozzarella cheese

freshly grated Parmesan cheese

1 cup cream or half-and-half, warmed

1. Preheat the oven to 350°F. Lightly oil a 2-quart gratin dish and put a moderately large pot of water on to boil.

2. Put 2 teaspoons oil in a skillet over medium heat and add the onion and sage. Cook, giving them an occasional stir, until soft and golden, about 12 minutes.

3. Meanwhile, peel the sweet potatoes, then slice them as thinly as you can manage. Salt the water, then drop them in. Allow the water to return to a boil, which may take a few minutes. Boil for a minute or until the potatoes are partly tender when pierced with a knife, then drain. Toss them with the onions, chopped parsley, and garlic.

4. Scoop a third of the potatoes into the prepared dish and even them out. Season with salt and pepper, add half the Gruyère, and grate over a little Parmesan. Repeat, making two more layers and covering the last with a dusting of the Parmesan. Pour the warm cream over all, cover with foil, and bake in the center of the oven for 25 minutes. Remove the foil and continue baking until the potatoes are utterly soft and the gratin has browned, another 25 minutes or so. Let the gratin stand a few minutes before serving. If you're not ready to eat, it can wait in the turned-off oven for another half hour.

savory pies and gratins

*vegetable stews
and braises*

Overall, I find that vegetable stews and braises are the most comfortable supper dishes to make. The pace they demand is leisurely and relaxing, unlike the brisk tempo of a stir-fry. The layering of ingredients proceeds in a reliable fashion, allowing you to begin with a base of onions and then go on to prepare and add the other elements. I especially enjoy the results that arise from this mingling of ingredients—the larger flavors, the fragrances.

Another thing that's particularly enjoyable to me about stews, ragouts, and braises is the accompaniments that attend these gently braised vegetables. There's a world of choice out there, starting with something as simple as toasted bread rubbed with a clove of garlic. Polenta is a natural foil for juicy vegetables, and if you use the double-boiler method on page 205, you can let it cook unattended. A semolina gratin (page 39) offers drama—and protein. Semolina pancakes, crêpes, rice timbales, popovers—even biscuits—all work as accompaniments. While each of these dishes features a particular accompaniment, they are easily interchangeable. The one dish I don't serve a starchy accompaniment with is the Bollito Misto on page 35, since it usually contains potatoes. However, even here you could include a few exotic pasta shapes, ravioli, or tortellini on the platter to round out the texture of the dish.

2

Asparagus and Mushrooms
in mushroom broth with tender white beans

The actual cooking of the mushrooms and asparagus goes quickly, so wait until your beans are cooked and the polenta is ready before you begin. (If you haven't time for polenta, serve this over toast or with pasta.)

Save this dish for special occasions, when you won't mind a little extra fuss. What better event to celebrate than the arrival in your market of local asparagus? Although fresh peas make an ideal partner for asparagus, they don't always appear in time, so I make this simple ragout with dried beans at the beginning of the season. My first choice is the pretty flageolet or any home-cooked bean that's waiting for me in the freezer. When pressed for time, you can use organic canned cannellini beans. Vegan if made with olive oil and no cheese.

This is a light dish even with the polenta, so plan an appetizer, such as crostini with chive-scented ricotta, perhaps a first-course vegetable salad, then splurge on a dessert of strawberries with a yeasted sugar cake. For wine, either a citrusy Giacosa Arneis white from the Piedmont or a fruity Giacosa Dolcetto would be good.

Polenta Cooked in the Double Boiler
(page 205) or instant polenta
$1^{1}/_{2}$ cups Mushroom Stock (page 209)
$1^{1}/_{2}$ pounds medium to large mushrooms,
such as cremini or small portobellos
2 tablespoons olive oil
sea salt and freshly ground pepper
1 bunch of scallions, including an inch of the
greens, minced
1 garlic clove, minced

$1^{1}/_{2}$ cups cooked flageolet or cannellini beans
or 1 15-ounce can, drained
$2^{1}/_{2}$ pounds asparagus, tough ends snapped
off and stalks peeled if thick, then soaked
for 15 minutes and rinsed
$1/_{2}$ cup Parmesan cheese freshly grated or
more to taste
1 tablespoon butter
herbs in season, such as snipped chives with
chopped basil, marjoram, or chervil

1. Start the polenta, then make the stock, adding any mushroom and asparagus trimmings to the pot as you work. If you're using portobellos, scrape out the gills with a spoon, then thickly slice them.

2. Heat 1 tablespoon of the olive oil in a wide sauté pan over medium heat. Add half the mushrooms, season with a few pinches of salt and pepper, and sauté until they're well colored, 4 to 5 minutes. Scrape the mushrooms onto a plate, add the remaining oil to the pan, and cook the second half of the mushrooms. Combine the mushrooms in the pan, add most of the scallions and the garlic, and cook for another minute. Then pour

in the stock and add the beans. Simmer until the mushrooms are tender, about 10 minutes, then turn off the heat and set aside.

3. Simmer the asparagus in salted water in a skillet until tender, about 8 minutes, drain, turn onto a clean towel, and wrap to absorb the moisture and keep it warm. Check the seasonings in the polenta and stir in the Parmesan cheese.

4. When ready to serve, add the butter and the remaining scallions to the mushrooms. Shuffle the pan to distribute the butter throughout the sauce. Spoon $\frac{1}{2}$ cup or so of the polenta into the center of the plate. Arrange the asparagus around it and spoon the mushrooms and their sauce over the polenta. Garnish with the herbs and serve.

Beet and Tomato Ragout
with twice-baked goat cheese soufflés and baby bok choy

Beets and goat cheese show up together so often that I've even had them paired in quesadillas. Here they meet in a beet ragout with goat cheese soufflés and baby bok choy. If your beet greens are plentiful and in good shape, use them instead of the bok choy.

The ragout can be made vegan by using oil rather than butter and replacing the goat cheese soufflé with black rice (page 207) or wild rice (page 207).

I might start this supper with a cream of leek soup and end with frisée salad. Sparkling Italian Prosecco or Spanish Cava will stand up to the high, lively notes of the beets.

Both the beets and the soufflés can be prepared in advance, so putting together what looks like a complex dish ends up being surprisingly straightforward. Make the soufflés through their first baking whenever it is convenient for you, but preferably the same day.

2 tablespoons butter

1 medium red onion, finely diced

1 tablespoon tomato paste

1 tablespoon brown sugar

2 tablespoons chopped tarragon

1 small garlic clove, minced

4 large red beets, peeled and cut into irregular ½-inch dice

1 cup diced tomatoes and their juices, fresh or canned

sea salt and freshly ground pepper

balsamic or aged red wine vinegar to taste

Twice-Baked Goat Cheese Soufflés (page 134), prepared up to the second baking

3 small baby bok choy, slivered lengthwise

1. Melt half the butter in a medium sauté pan. Add the onion and cook over medium heat, stirring frequently, until it starts to color, about 7 minutes. Stir in the tomato paste, sugar, a few pinches of the tarragon, the garlic, and 1 cup water. Simmer until the onions are soft and the liquid is well reduced, about 20 minutes. Add the beets and tomatoes, season with ½ teaspoon salt, or more to taste, and some pepper. Cook until the beets are tender, about 25 minutes, adding more water as needed so that there is a little sauce at the end. Add 2 teaspoons or more of the vinegar and 1 tablespoon of the tarragon.

2. Twenty minutes before serving, remove the soufflés from the refrigerator and preheat the oven to 350°F. Bake the soufflés for the second time until golden and hot, 15 to 20 minutes. Simmer the bok choy in a skillet of salted water until tender, about 5 minutes, then pour off the water, add the rest of the butter and a pinch of the remaining tarragon, and cover to keep warm. Reheat the beets.

3. To serve, spoon the beets onto each plate along with any juices, then lift the soufflés out of their baking dish with a spatula and nestle them in the beets. Add greens to each plate and garnish with the rest of the chopped tarragon.

Chickpeas and Chard
with cilantro and cumin

I happen to like a lot of chard in proportion to the chickpeas, but you can use half this amount. Red or other colored stems make the dish especially attractive. Vegan as is.

This is a substantial dish so you don't need much else—a pureed red pepper soup to start or a spunky green salad at the end. A spicy white wine, such as a Spanish Albariño, would work with these Mediterranean flavors.

2 tablespoons olive oil

1 large onion, finely diced

pinch or 2 of saffron threads

2 garlic cloves

sea salt and freshly ground pepper

1 cup cilantro leaves

$1/4$ cup parsley leaves

$1/2$ teaspoon ground cumin or more to taste

2 teaspoons tomato paste

14 chard leaves (2 medium bunches) with stems

2 15-ounce cans chickpeas, preferably organic, with liquid, or 3 cups home-cooked

1. Heat 1 tablespoon plus 1 teaspoon of the olive oil in a wide skillet. Add the onion and saffron. Cook over medium heat, stirring occasionally, for 12 to 15 minutes. Meanwhile, pound the garlic with $1/2$ teaspoon salt, the cilantro, parsley, and cumin to make a rough paste. When the onions are golden and soft, add the paste to the pan along with the tomato paste and work it into the onions.

2. Slice the chard leaves off their stems. Put them in a wide pot with 2 cups water and cook, covered, until wilted and tender, about 5 minutes. Set the leaves aside in a colander, reserving the cooking water.

3. Trim the chard stems so that you're left with planklike pieces of even width. Cut the planks into strips, then into fine dice and drop them into the reserved chard water. Simmer until tender, about 10 minutes, then turn off the heat.

4. Add the chickpeas to the onion with their liquid or 1 cup water or stock. Coarsely chop the chard and add it as well. Simmer for 10 minutes, then add the stems. Taste for salt and season with pepper. Serve with the remaining oil drizzled over all.

Bollito Misto of Vegetables

Bollito misto refers to an Italian way of cooking meats, but it's a great concept for vegetables, too. While "boiled mixed vegetables" could sound a bit depressing, a panoply of produce in its season is forever beautiful, its perfume sweet and clean. Plus, this is the least taxing and most delightful dish to make. Serve it simply with good olive oil and fresh herbs, a more elaborate salsa verde, or an herb butter. Depending on the sauce, the dish is vegan.

Serve a bollito misto with good chewy bread and start the meal with a goat cheese soufflé (page 132) or end it with a cheese course. For wines, an Old World Chardonnay with minerality and restraint, such as Pouilly-Fuissé from the Mâcon, or a Pinot Noir from Côte Chalonnaise would make a good partner.

Plan on ¾ pound or more vegetables per person. Leftovers can be turned into a salad or joined with their broth to make a soup. You needn't have a lot of different vegetables—even a few are sufficient, and it can be a little of this or a lot of that.

A Summer Bollito Misto with Olive Oil

FOR THE BROTH

several slivered garlic cloves

a few scallions or 1 onion, sliced

1 teaspoon peppercorns

several parsley and thyme sprigs

2 teaspoons olive oil

2 teaspoons sea salt

FOR THE VEGETABLES

new potatoes with rose or yellow flesh, such as Huckleberry or Yellow Finn, scrubbed and sliced about ⅜ inch thick

small market carrots, scrubbed and halved lengthwise

fennel bulbs, trimmed and quartered, joined at the base

celery ribs, peeled and cut into sections (include some of the leaves in the broth)

leeks, halved lengthwise but joined at the root, washed well

small summer turnips, peeled or not, halved or quartered

summer squash, sliced about ⅜ inch thick in rounds or lengths

green beans, tipped and tailed

red and purple radishes, scrubbed, with a few leaves left attached

shucked and peeled fava beans or peas

vegetable stews and braises

your favorite extra virgin olive oil

Malden sea salt or fleur de sel

freshly ground pepper

chopped fresh herbs in season—one of the many kinds of basil available, marjoram, dill, lemon thyme, tarragon, etc.

1. Simmer 2 to 3 quarts water in 2 wide skillets, each with a flotilla of sliced garlic, scallions or sliced onion, peppercorns, parsley and thyme sprigs, a teaspoon of olive oil, and a teaspoon of sea salt.

2. Use one pan for "difficult" vegetables, such as those that bleed (radishes) or aromatic cruciferous vegetables (radishes again and turnips). Use the other pan for the more neutral potatoes, carrots, squash, and celery. Start with the longest-cooking vegetables, such as potatoes and carrots, then add the quicker-cooking ones, such as zucchini, as you go along. Don't worry about each vegetable being utterly perfect. You can always remove them individually as they finish cooking.

3. When the vegetables are done, arrange them on a platter. Pour over a little of the broth from the pan in which the potatoes cooked. Spoon your best olive oil over all, and season with the sea salt, pepper, and chopped herbs.

A Winter Bollito Misto with Mustard-Herb Butter

A bollito misto for a winter supper will include more robust vegetables and a robust sauce to match, in this case a mustard butter. Look to spiraled broccoli Romanesco and cauliflower, cut into bite-sized florets; storage turnips, thickly peeled and cut into wedges; thin rounds of peeled Delicata squash; buttery yellow rutabagas, also thinly sliced; and pear onions. Broccoli stems, once peeled, make a delicate and gorgeous addition. Leeks, celery, fennel, and boiling potatoes, which are found in both seasons, can be included as well. Simmer the vegetables in water with the aromatics—they will take a little longer than summer vegetables—then serve them with the following butter dabbed over the top.

Mustard-Herb Butter

4 tablespoons soft butter

2 teaspoons prepared mustard, fine or grainy, or more to taste

a small handful of mixed herbs, such as lemon thyme, chives, tarragon, parsley, oregano

1 teaspoon finely grated lemon zest

sea salt and freshly ground pepper to taste

Mix all the ingredients together.

SERVES 4

Braised Fennel
with a saffron rice timbale

The fennel can be cooked hours before you plan to eat, then heated and the pan deglazed, at no cost to its quality. Start the rice after you have your vegetable base started. It will hold its heat in the pan while the vegetables cook.

A saffron rice timbale surrounded with this braised fennel makes a handsome center-piece for a meal. The timbales are easily formed. Just pack the hot rice into a ramekin, then turn it onto the plate—a simple gesture that provides focus for a main dish. With a substitute for the butter, this dish is vegan.

In summer, start this supper with an appetizer of roasted peppers and tomatoes baked with herbs and capers and finish with a salad of soft, delicate butterhead lettuces dressed with a lemon vinaigrette. For wine, consider an unoaked Calera Viognier or a Domaine Tempier Bandol rosé.

2 tablespoons olive oil

1 carrot, finely diced

$^1/_2$ onion, finely diced

1 celery rib, finely diced

several thyme sprigs or $^1/_4$ teaspoon dried

1 bay leaf

1 tablespoon tomato paste

1 cup dry white wine

sea salt and freshly ground pepper

Saffron Rice (page 206)

3 large fennel bulbs, quartered but attached at the core, plus 3 tablespoons greens, chopped

4 basil leaves

1 tablespoon butter

1. Heat half the oil in a large skillet over medium-high heat and add the carrot, onion, celery, thyme, and bay leaf. Sauté until the onion begins to color, about 5 minutes, then work in the tomato paste and cook it a bit. Add half the wine and reduce until syrupy. Season with salt and pepper, then scrape everything into a bowl.

2. Start cooking the rice.

3. Brown the fennel in the rest of the oil over medium heat, turning every so often, about 15 minutes. Add the diced vegetables back to the pan, tear the basil leaves over all, add a tablespoon of the fennel greens, and pour in 1 cup water. Cover and cook until the liquid has evaporated, 10 to 12 minutes. When the pan is dry, add another ½ cup water and continue cooking until the fennel is tender when pierced with a knife, 15 to 20 minutes. Leave a little liquid in the pan.

4. Transfer the fennel and vegetables to a platter, then return the pan to the stove, turn the heat to high, and add the remaining wine and the butter. Scrape the caramelized bits of debris from the pan. When the wine and butter have reduced by half, add the rest of the chopped fennel greens, taste for salt, and season with pepper.

5. Scoop portions of rice into a cup or a ramekin, then turn each out onto a plate. Spoon the vegetables around the rice and drizzle with the pan sauce.

A Platter of Braised Green Vegetables
with a semolina gratin

SERVES 4

Golden, puffed, and ever so tender, the gratin is based on the recipe for semolina gnocchi but uses whole eggs instead of just the yolks, making it more like a pudding-soufflé—and more protein-dense. Since the gratin is on the rich side, I've made the braised vegetables the main element in this dish. Indeed, they are eye-catching and palate-catching, too. But the gratin is the foil that sets them off. In fact, it flatters all kinds of vegetable dishes—a mushroom stew would be divine, and so would something as simple as roasted asparagus.

While the oven is heating, make the gratin batter. Then, while it's baking, cook the vegetables. Both should be ready at about the same time.

vegetable stews and braises

To complete the meal, nothing more than a crunchy appetizer is needed—salted almonds, crudités, or a radish crostini to start—and a salad to follow. For wine, choose a slightly chilled lighter-bodied red, such as a Beaujolais or Valpolicella.

THE GRATIN

3½ cups milk

sea salt

1 cup semolina

4 eggs

½ to 1 cup grated Gruyère or Fontina cheese

½ cup freshly grated Parmesan cheese

2 tablespoons butter, melted

THE VEGETABLES

1 tablespoon olive oil, plus extra to finish

1 tablespoon butter

1 onion, thinly sliced

pinch of saffron threads

¼ teaspoon fennel seeds, crushed

1 large fennel bulb, halved lengthwise and sliced lengthwise into eighths

½ cup dry white wine

sea salt and freshly ground pepper

10 basil leaves

4 zucchini (about 1 pound), sliced lengthwise into ribbons about ¼ inch thick

8 tender chard leaves, stems discarded and leaves cut into wide ribbons

1. Lightly butter a 3-quart gratin or lasagne dish. Preheat the oven to 350°F. Heat the milk in a spacious saucepan with 1 teaspoon salt. When it's almost boiling, whisk in the semolina. Stir constantly as the milk comes to a boil, then lower the heat and cook until thick, about 5 minutes. Remove from the heat.

2. Whisk the eggs with some of the hot semolina, then vigorously stir them back into the pot. Add the Gruyère and half the Parmesan. Pour the batter into the prepared dish, drizzle with the melted butter, and sprinkle with the rest of the Parmesan. Bake until puffed, bubbling, and golden on top, 40 to 50 minutes.

3. Meanwhile, heat the oil and butter in a wide skillet. Add the onion, saffron, fennel seeds, and fennel. Cook over medium-high heat for a few minutes to heat everything up, then add the wine. Season with $\frac{1}{2}$ teaspoon salt and a few twists of the pepper mill and tear a few of the basil leaves over all. Lower the heat and cook until the fennel and onions are translucent and the wine has reduced to a glaze, about 5 minutes. If the pan gets dry, add more wine or water.

4. Lay the zucchini over the fennel, drizzle with olive oil, season with salt and pepper, and add a few more basil leaves. Cover with the chard, add another $\frac{1}{2}$ cup water, then cover and cook until the zucchini is tender, about 7 minutes. If you allow the liquid to cook away, the fennel and onions will brown beautifully. If you want it more delicate, then make sure the pan has some liquid.

5. Gently turn the vegetables in their pan and then spoon them onto a platter with their juices. Shred the remaining basil leaves over all and season with pepper. Serve with a mound of the gratin, being sure to include lots of the golden crust.

Porcini and Tomato Ragout
with polenta

SERVES 4

In northern New Mexico, the porcini appear just as the tomatoes do, in the rainy season of late summer, and a dish that brings them together makes good culinary sense. As good as they are, though, our wild mushrooms don't seem to have the intensity that Italian porcini possess, so I always include some dried Italian mushrooms in the dish to boost that wild flavor. Without the final addition of Parmesan, this ragout is vegan.

Begin this meal with a vegetable salad, such as a shredded salad of many greens, beets with ricotta salata and olives, or warm green beans with an herb vinaigrette. For wine, try an Italian red, medium bodied with acidity—such as a Barbera or Chianti Classico.

The ragout itself doesn't take long to make, and it can be reheated, but start with the polenta, remembering that the double-boiler method takes over an hour, though not your attention. To make the most of your expensive dried mushrooms, soak them for at least a half hour in warm water before using and plan to use the liquid as your cooking medium.

Polenta Cooked in the Double Boiler

(page 205)

$^1/_2$ to 1 ounce dried porcini

3 tablespoons olive oil

1 small onion, finely diced

2 tablespoons chopped parsley

1 tablespoon finely chopped rosemary

1 garlic clove, finely chopped

2 teaspoons tomato paste

$^1/_2$ cup red wine

sea salt and freshly ground pepper

1$^1/_2$ pounds large fresh mushrooms, ideally porcini or a mixture of different varieties, the gills still closed if possible, thickly sliced

4 large tomatoes, peeled, seeded, and diced, or 1 15-ounce can diced tomatoes

Parmigiano-Reggiano for grating

1. Start the polenta. Cover the dried mushrooms with 2 cups warm water and set aside for at least 30 minutes, while you assemble and chop the rest of the ingredients. When you're ready to start cooking, pour the mushroom-soaking liquid through a fine strainer and coarsely chop the reconstituted mushrooms.

2. Heat a third of the oil in a wide nonstick skillet or braising pan. Add the onion and the drained porcini. Cook over medium-high heat until the onion is well colored, about 7 minutes, then add half the herbs and garlic and work in the tomato paste. Add the wine and let it reduce to a syrupy consistency. Season with salt and pepper and remove to a bowl.

3. Without rinsing the pan, add the rest of the oil and, when hot, add the fresh mushrooms. Cook over high heat until they start to color nicely, release, and then begin to reabsorb their juices, about 8 minutes. Season them with several big pinches of salt, then add the onion and the tomatoes and pour in the strained mushroom liquid. Reduce the heat to medium-low and simmer until the mushrooms are cooked, at least 15 minutes. If a great deal of juice has been given off by the wild mushrooms, pour it into a separate pan, bring to a boil, and reduce until about $^1/_2$ cup remains. (Whisk in a spoonful of butter if you'd like the added richness.)

4. Add the remaining herbs and garlic to the ragout. Spoon a mound of polenta onto individual plates, make a depression in the surface, and spoon the mushrooms on top. Spoon the juice around the polenta and grate a little of the cheese over all.

Variation   Make a hearty rustic dish by serving the ragout, with its juices, over big slabs of toasted hearth bread that has been rubbed lightly with garlic, brushed with oil, and broken into large shards. Add thin shavings of the Parmesan and serve.

Brussels Sprout and Mushroom Ragout
with herb dumplings

Simultaneously homey and special, this ragout has proven to more than one person that Brussels sprouts are good. While the recipe is made easier by using sliced onions, it becomes more special if you include pearl onions, cipollini, or whole shallots, peeled first and cooked in place of the yellow onions. And although you may be tempted to use commercial gnocchi, dumplings are insanely easy to make and involve about 1 minute of your time, so do give them a try. Italian wild mushroom bouillon (Star brand) makes a passable alternative—or addition—to your own stock, but it can be salty, so be sure you taste it and dilute it if need be.

I would start this meal with something raw and fresh, such as a grated carrot salad with mint and black olives or a more substantial salad of bulgur and green lentils with chickpeas, with a walnut vinaigrette. A leaf salad might follow, along with a dessert, such as a caramelized apple tart with cinnamon custard. For wine, try a New World Chardonnay with rich fruit and a little oak, from Santa Barbara, such as Sanford or Au Bon Climat.

Start with the stock, whether bouillon or made from scratch. While it's simmering, start the onions and mushrooms, blanch the sprouts, and get the dumpling ingredients together. Once the vegetables and stock are combined, make the dumpling batter. Drop the batter into the pot, and it's a matter of 10 minutes before the dish is ready. The ragout is vegan, but not the dumplings. Wild rice, however, would be delicious in their place.

Mushroom Stock (page 209)

4 teaspoons olive oil

2 medium to large onions, sliced about ½ inch thick

¾ pound white mushrooms, cremini, shiitake, or a mixture, rinsed and sliced thickly on a diagonal

3 tablespoons chopped parsley

1 tablespoon chopped tarragon

1 plump garlic clove, minced

½ large lemon

1 pound Brussels sprouts, halved or quartered

1 cup all-purpose flour

1 teaspoon baking powder

⅜ teaspoon sea salt

¾ cup milk, heated with 3 tablespoons butter or oil

3 tablespoons mixed chopped parsley and tarragon

1 egg

HERB DUMPLINGS

vegetable stews and braises

1. Make the mushroom stock. Once it's simmering, bring a pot of water to a boil for the Brussels sprouts.

2. Heat the oil in a wide nonstick skillet. Add the onions and cook over medium heat, stirring frequently, until aromatic and nicely colored, about 12 minutes. Meanwhile, slice the mushrooms and chop the herbs and garlic.

3. Once the onions are a rich color, raise the heat to high and add the mushrooms, herbs, and garlic to the pan. Squeeze the lemon juice over the mushrooms and sauté until the mushrooms are browned in places, 5 to 7 minutes, then reduce the heat to low.

4. Add salt to the boiling water, then the Brussels sprouts along with any loose leaves. Boil until nearly tender, 4 to 6 minutes, depending on size. Check by piercing them with a paring knife. Drain, then add them to the pan and pour in the mushroom stock. At this point you can turn off the heat and let the vegetables stand until you're ready to make the dumplings.

5. For the dumplings, mix the flour with the baking powder and salt. Pour in the milk, herbs, and egg and stir quickly together with a fork. Add the dumpling batter by spoonfuls to the ragout, making 12 small dumplings in all. You'll have extra batter, but don't use it or the dish will be too bready. (It's hard to make the batter in smaller amounts.) Cover the pan with tented foil, bring everything to a simmer, and cook for 10 minutes. Serve in soup plates, with 3 dumplings in each bowl.

Ratatouille
with spongy semolina crêpes

I hadn't made ratatouille for years—I was too busy making other things. But sitting down once again to this silky stew was like settling in with an old friend. If you're not in a rush, ratatouille is pure pleasure to make. It wants nurturing and in turn is relaxing to assemble. The various small tasks stack up nicely and can mostly be done while the onions are slowly melting. You might as well make plenty, because given a day or two, ratatouille only gets better. Cold, it makes a delicious member of the mezze plate, (see page 162), and leftovers can also go into a frittata, a pasta, or on top of a pizza or bruschetta. Served hot, it's good with these unusual spongy semolina crêpes or saffron rice. The ratatouille is vegan, but the pancakes are not.

Given all the vegetables in a ratatouille, you might start your meal with something uncomplicated, such as baked ricotta with thyme or crostini with spicy tapenade and goat cheese. For dessert, I'd offer a plate of fresh figs and raspberries with a Muscat sabayon. And for wine, a Provençal rosé would be a classic choice.

I used to sauté each vegetable separately over high heat before bringing them together, a workable but slightly harried method. I now prefer the calmer approach of stewing the onions and roasting or grilling the peppers before adding them to the mix. This is hardly a compromise, for the results are unquestionably good.

Because the semolina crêpes are made with yeast, they need 1½ hours to rise. But the batter can be started earlier in the day or the day before.

6 tablespoons olive oil	6 zucchini, about 1½ pounds, quartered
2 large onions, thinly sliced	lengthwise and cut into 3-inch lengths
2 medium eggplants (about 1½ pounds),	2 thyme branches
cut into 1-inch cubes	6 large basil leaves, torn into pieces
sea salt and freshly ground pepper	3 marjoram or oregano sprigs
5 tomatoes, peeled and seeded	Spongy Semolina Crêpes (recipe follows) or
3 to 4 thick-fleshed bell peppers, red and	Saffron Rice (page 206)
yellow	minced parsley for garnish

1. Warm 1 tablespoon of the oil in a Dutch oven. Add the onions and stir. Cover the pot, reduce the heat to low, and cook for 30 minutes, stirring occasionally, while you prepare the rest of the vegetables. Toward the end, they should be soft, a bit juicy, and not at all browned.

2. While the onions are cooking, toss the eggplant with 1 teaspoon salt and set aside. Cut the tomatoes into 1-inch pieces. Char the peppers all over (under the broiler or in an open flame), then drop them into a plastic bag to steam for 15 minutes. Wipe off the burned skin, remove the seeds, and slice into lengths a scant ½ inch wide.

3. When the onions are ready, heat 1 tablespoon of the remaining oil in a wide skillet over high heat and sauté the zucchini until golden in places, about 5 minutes. Add the zucchini to the pot along with the peppers.

4. Give the eggplant a quick rinse, then wrap it in a towel and press to wick up the moisture. Heat the remaining oil in the same skillet. Add the eggplant, stir immediately, and then sauté over medium-high heat until nicely colored, 8 to 10 minutes. Add it to the onions, followed by the tomatoes. Season with 1 teaspoon salt and add the herbs. Cover and cook very gently over very low heat.

5. When the vegetables are tender, after 30 minutes or so, remove the lid and raise the heat to reduce the juices to a thick sauce, gently turning the vegetables as the juices

vegetable stews and braises

47

bubble. If there is a great deal of juice, pour it into a saucepan and reduce until covered with bubbles and thickened, then pour it back in the pot. Taste for salt and season with pepper.

6. Make the crêpes and serve them with the vegetables. Or make the rice, press it into a ramekin or teacup, then turn it out onto the plate, surround with the vegetables, and garnish with a bit of fresh minced parsley.

Spongy Semolina Crêpes

Yeast gives these crêpes texture, tenderness, and big spongy bubbles, but it does mean that you need to make the batter at least 1½ hours ahead of time or the day before.

1½ teaspoons active dry yeast

1 cup semolina flour

1 cup whole wheat pastry flour or
   unbleached all-purpose flour

½ teaspoon sea salt

1 teaspoon sugar or sugar substitute

1 tablespoon sunflower seed oil or olive oil

2 eggs

1¾ cups water

2 pinches of saffron threads steeped in 2
   tablespoons boiling water for 5 minutes

1. Stir the yeast into ¼ cup warm water and set aside.

2. Put the flours, salt, sugar, oil, eggs, and water in a blender. Blend on high, stopping once or twice to scrape down the sides. Pour the batter into a bowl and stir in the yeast. Cover and set aside to rise for at least 1½ hours or overnight in the refrigerator. Stir in the steeped saffron threads just before cooking.

3. Place an 8-inch nonstick skillet with a little butter or oil over medium heat. When the pan is hot, pour in ¼ cup batter. Give the pan a swirl with your wrist to distribute the batter over the surface, then cook until the surface is covered with bubbles and the bottom is set and golden, about 2 minutes. Turn the crêpe and cook the second side until set, a minute or less. Stack the finished crêpes on top of one another as they finish cooking and they will hold their heat.

Winter Squash Green Curry
with mushrooms, eggplant, and tofu

Choose a butternut squash with a nice long neck—it's the easiest to work with. Begin by salting the eggplant and soaking the mushrooms, then make the curry paste so that the flavors have time to marry. Drain the tofu, peel and chunk the squash, and just before cooking, slice the revived mushrooms.

Seasonally speaking, winter squash and eggplant may not sound like a match. But the first winter squash comes into season while the eggplant is far from finished, so in fact they overlap quite nicely. Add tofu and dried shiitake mushrooms and you have a deep-flavored autumn stew that happens to be vegan. You can add the tofu uncooked to the sauce or brown it first in a nonstick skillet to give it a little more oomph. (You can also leave it out if you don't like tofu.)

I always like curries with rice—a delicate brown or white basmati or a floral jasmine rice. A passion fruit and pineapple fool would make a cool tropical dessert. And for wine, try a spicy dry Gewürztraminer from the Alsace such as Zind Humbrecht.

THE CURRY PASTE

3 to 4 large garlic cloves, coarsely chopped

1 heaping tablespoon peeled and coarsely chopped fresh ginger

3 stalks lemon grass, centers only, minced, or 2 tablespoons frozen lemon grass

3 to 4 jalapeño chiles, to taste, seeded and chopped

2 shallots, chopped (about $\frac{1}{3}$ cup) or $\frac{1}{3}$ cup chopped scallion or onion

$\frac{1}{2}$ cup finely chopped cilantro stems or leaves

$\frac{1}{2}$ teaspoon freshly ground black pepper

1 teaspoon ground cumin

2 teaspoons ground coriander

1 teaspoon salt

zest and juice of 1 lime

THE EGGPLANT,
SQUASH, AND TOFU

2 small oblong eggplants (4 to 6 ounces each)

sea salt

8 dried shiitake mushrooms, covered with $1\frac{1}{2}$ cups boiling water

3 tablespoons roasted peanut oil or mixed roasted and light oil

1 small butternut squash (about $1\frac{1}{4}$ pounds), peeled and cut into $\frac{3}{4}$-inch chunks

1 can unsweetened coconut milk

1 block firm tofu packed in water, drained and cut into 1-inch cubes

6 Thai basil leaves, plus sprigs for garnish, if available

fresh lime juice to taste

1. Put everything for the curry paste in the small work bowl of a food processor and work until pastelike and smooth. Add a little extra lime juice or water to loosen the mixture if necessary. Set aside.

2. Quarter the eggplant lengthwise and cut into ¾-inch wedges. Sprinkle with salt and set it aside while you prepare everything else. Just before you're ready to cook, remove the mushrooms from their soaking water, squeeze out (but save) their juices, and cut them into quarters or wide strips, discarding the tough stem. Reserve the liquid.

3. Heat 1 tablespoon of the oil in a wide skillet. Rinse the eggplant, blot it dry, then add it to the pan and turn it quickly in the oil. Cook over medium-high heat just to brown the cut surfaces, 4 to 5 minutes.

4. Heat the remaining oil in a wide Dutch oven. Add the squash and cook over medium-high heat, turning every so often, until caramelized in places after several minutes. Add the eggplant, reduce the heat to medium, then pour in the coconut milk, mushroom-soaking water, mushrooms, and two-thirds of the curry paste. Cover and simmer for 15 minutes or until the squash is tender, by which time the sauce will have lost its color.

5. Add the tofu and basil leaves, then simmer until the tofu is heated through, about 5 minutes. Taste for salt, adding more if needed, along with the lime juice. Just before serving, stir in the rest of the curry paste and garnish with sprigs of basil.

Asparagus Ragout
for a transitional season

This ragout is on my menu when I'm ready for spring but it's not altogether ready for me. In this transitional dish, the peas and asparagus are the link to spring, but the rest of the vegetables—carrots, rainbow chard, mushrooms—hang back a bit, still in winter.

As this is not a hefty stew, you'll want to include a more substantial component in your meal, but make it something that doesn't need any of your attention—baked ricotta cheese with pepper and thyme or the sautéed cheese on page 166. Or you might consider slipping a few cooked ravioli into the stew at the end. Serve a Sonoma Sauvignon Blanc. It will stand up to the asparagus and the beurre blanc.

THE BEURRE BLANC

$^1/_4$ cup white wine vinegar or Champagne vinegar

$^1/_4$ cup dry white wine or Champagne

2 tablespoons finely diced shallot

sea salt and freshly ground pepper

6 to 8 tablespoons cold butter, cut into small pieces

THE RAGOUT

1 bunch rainbow chard, with stems

sea salt and freshly ground pepper

2 tablespoons butter

5 teaspoons olive oil

$^1/_3$ cup finely diced onion or leek

8 to 12 slender carrots, halved lengthwise

$^1/_2$ cup dry white wine

$1^1/_2$ pounds asparagus, the tough ends snapped off, thick stalks peeled and cut into 3-inch lengths

$^1/_4$ pound edible-pod peas and/or snow peas, trimmed

$^3/_4$ pound fresh shiitake or cremini mushrooms, stems removed, the larger caps quartered or halved, the smaller ones left whole

2 tablespoons minced chervil or a mixture of parsley and tarragon

Cooking the several parts separately results in a beautifully orchestrated dish. The beurre blanc can be made at any convenient moment and set aside. The carrots, asparagus, and peas are cooked together. The chard is added to each serving, and the mushrooms, which crown the dish, are sautéed separately. This is far easier to accomplish than it sounds. The most important thing to avoid is having the asparagus and peas sit too long while waiting for the mushrooms— you don't want them to lose their luster.

1. To make the beurre blanc, put the vinegar, wine, shallot, and a pinch of salt in a small saucepan and simmer until only 2 tablespoons remain. Turn off the heat and whisk in the butter piece by piece until all is incorporated. The sauce should be thick and white. Season with a little pepper and set aside.

2. To make the ragout, slice the leaves off the chard stems, wash well, then cut into ribbons about an inch wide. Trim the stems so that you have even planks, then cut them into strips about 3/8 inch wide and 3 inches long. Bring 2 to 3 cups water to a boil, add a few pinches of salt, and simmer the chard stems until nearly tender, about 5 minutes. Lay the leaves over the top and cook them until tender, about 5 minutes. Set aside.

3. Heat 1 tablespoon each of the butter and oil in a wide skillet fitted with a lid. Add the onion and carrots. Cook over medium-high heat for a few minutes just to brown things a bit, then reduce the heat to medium. Add the wine, let most of it sizzle away, then add 1 cup water and the asparagus. Season with a few pinches of salt, then lower the heat even more, cover, and cook until the asparagus and carrots are nearly tender, about 6 minutes. Add the peas. In all, this should take about 8 minutes.

4. Heat the remaining butter and oil in a wide skillet over high heat. When the butter foams, add the mushrooms and quickly stir them about. Sauté until the mushrooms have browned nicely, then released and partially reabsorbed their juices, reducing the heat to medium once they've colored, about 8 minutes. Season with salt and pepper to taste.

5. Taste each part of the dish for salt. Loosely arrange the vegetables into 4 pasta bowls. Distribute the chard and chard stems among them, then spoon several tablespoons of juice into each. Add a dollop of beurre blanc to each bowl, cover with the mushrooms, then garnish with the minced herbs and serve.

vegetable stews
and braises

pasta with
vegetables

*P*asta has long been the fallback position for the harried cook. But once we got nervous about carbohydrates and suspected that it was true that pasta does make you fat, it began to lose favor. I probably eat it only once every few weeks myself, but I love pasta, and now that it's no longer a stopgap kind of meal it has become something special to look forward to. I have, however, changed my approach to pasta dishes. These pasta dishes are full of vegetables. The penne with masses of broccoli, for example, uses two full pounds of broccoli, along with pine nuts and olives, while the summer lasagne pairs ½ pound of noodles with 2½ pounds of zucchini. So these recipes are vegetable dishes as much as they are pasta dishes.

I also use less oil than I used to. And whole wheat pasta appears far more frequently now, except on those occasions when a white flour–egg pasta is just the ticket. How we got it in our heads that whole wheat pasta is heavy and dull beats me, but I suspect that it comes from those days when so many so-called health foods were earnest but stodgy. Today's whole wheat pasta possesses a light, nutty presence that is especially pleasing with strong foods like broccoli. An organic whole wheat pasta I use frequently is called Bionaturae, an Italian brand that's easy to find in larger natural food stores. It's on the lighter side of whole wheat, while DeCecco's whole wheat spaghetti is darker and more robust. When I want to splurge on something really special that has a rich, warm flavor, I go for pasta made from farro (spelt), a wheatlike grain.

When it comes to making lasagne, no-boil noodles make forming a lasagne so much easier that it can put lasagne on the supper menu with some regularity. The whole tedious business of parboiling is simply skipped—and they're good. Of course nothing is as good as a lasagne made with thin sheets of fresh pasta, but that qualifies as a special dinner dish.

3

Whole Wheat Penne
with masses of broccoli, green olives, and pine nuts

When I can get my hands on fresh sweet broccoli from the farmers' market, I like to use lots of it, including any leaves that remain on the stalks. They're sweet and delicious, and there's no reason not to use them.

The caramelized onions, pine nuts, and green olives offer the lively, assertive flavors that go so well with broccoli. If you eat anchovies, mash 5 or 6 into the onions once they've colored up—they boost the savor of this dish amazingly. Without anchovies or the final grating of Parmesan cheese, this dish is vegan.

For wine, choose a Zinfandel from Sonoma, such as Ridge Geyserville, or an Oregon Pinot Gris from King Estate.

2 large onions, cut into $1/2$-inch dice	sea salt and freshly ground pepper
4 teaspoons olive oil, plus extra for the pasta	2 pounds broccoli, cut into small florets, stems peeled and diced
2 garlic cloves, finely chopped	
$1/2$ cup pine nuts, toasted in a dry skillet	$3/4$ to 1 pound whole wheat penne, snails, or shells
$3/4$ cup pitted green olives, roughly chopped	
$1/3$ cup chopped marjoram or oregano	a chunk of Parmesan cheese for the table

1. Cook the onions in the oil in a wide skillet over medium-low heat, stirring occasionally. When they're golden, after 30 minutes or so, add the garlic, pine nuts, olives, and marjoram and turn the heat to low. Taste for salt and season with pepper.

2. Bring a large pot of water to a boil, add salt, then throw in the broccoli florets and stems and cook just until they're tender but retain a little bite, about 5 minutes. Scoop them out and add them to the pan with the onions along with a little of the water.

3. Add the pasta to the boiling water. When it's done, drain it into a colander, then return it to the pot and toss it with additional olive oil to taste, salt, and pepper. Divide among heated pasta bowls, then cover with the vegetables. Pass the cheese at the table for those who wish it.

Gnocchi
with winter squash and seared radicchio

I'm hopeless when it comes to making gnocchi, but if you're not, homemade will be the best. However, if gnocchi is a challenge for you, in its place, use store-bought, or ricotta ravioli, mushroom tortellini, or wide flat egg noodles. Vegans will want to use dried pasta and omit any cheese.

I've made this recipe many times, and this is the simplest version. While I've opted for steaming the squash, another way to go is to brown it slowly in olive oil with plenty of the fresh sage and garlic, which adds another layer of flavor and a firmer texture, although the volume shrinks considerably.

A hearty red wine is called for here. A Napa Valley Merlot such as Joseph Phelps or a Petite Syrah from Stag's Leap Winery would be an excellent match.

Start with a utilitarian butternut squash, which has that great, easy-to-handle neck. Use the neck for the cubes and the base on another occasion. Cook the radicchio while the squash is steaming, then simmer the gnocchi in the same water used to steam the squash. Finally, bring everything together. If time allows, you can make a thin, vibrant sauce from the trimmings to spoon around the dish.

1 large butternut squash (about 3 pounds)

¼ cup olive oil

sea salt and freshly ground pepper

1 head radicchio, sliced into wide ribbons

2 garlic cloves

a big handful of parsley leaves

12 or more large sage leaves or 1 tablespoon chopped rosemary

1 tablespoon butter if making the sauce

¾ to 1 pound potato gnocchi, cheese ravioli, or mushroom tortellini, homemade or store-bought

freshly grated Parmigiano-Reggiano and/or crumbled Gorgonzola cheese

1. Cut off the neck of the squash, divide into two or three easily managed sections, and slice off the skin. Cut into slabs, then dice into ½-inch cubes. (Don't worry about irregular shapes!) Toss with a little olive oil and sea salt, then steam over 3 cups simmering water until tender, about 20 minutes. Reserve the water.

2. Heat 2 tablespoons of the remaining oil in a wide skillet; add the radicchio, season with salt, and cook over medium-high heat, stirring occasionally, until wilted, tender, and no longer red, about 8 minutes. When the squash is done, add it to the pan. Chop the garlic, parsley, and sage together. Add most of it to the radicchio and squash and reserve the rest.

3. If you have time to make a sauce, put the strings and seeds from the squash in a pan with 2 cups of the water that was used to steam the squash, a few pinches of salt,

pasta with vegetables

and any leftover bits of parsley, garlic, squash, and sage. Simmer, partially covered, for 20 minutes, then strain. Whisk in a tablespoon of butter and you have a beautiful, thin orange sauce to spoon around the pasta.

4. Salt a skillet of water, bring to a boil, add the gnocchi, and simmer until done. Add them to the pan with a little of the cooking water. Taste for salt, season with pepper, and add the remaining herbs and garlic. Serve with the remaining oil drizzled over the top, plain, or with the cheese or cheeses.

Winter Squash Lasagne
with sage, walnuts, and black kale

SERVES 6

Begin with the béchamel sauce so that the milk can absorb the flavor of the aromatics, then turn to chopping the squash, onion, and herbs. While the squash is cooking, finish the sauce and compose the dish. You don't need to cook the kale until 30 minutes or so before serving.

Lasagne is seldom fast to put together, but it's always just right for a weekend supper with friends and family. I adore winter squash, so when I wanted to use it in a lasagne, I started playing with it, adding walnuts for their texture and taste and Gruyère cheese for the way it echoes the nuts. I keep the layering simple but serve each square on a bed of garlicky black kale, or other variety of kale.

Serve this big handsome dish with an Old Vine Sonoma Zinfandel such as Ridge's Lytton Springs or a Chianti Classico. Fonterutoli would be a good choice.

$3^{1}/_{2}$ cups milk

aromatics: 1 garlic clove, 1 slice onion, 1 bay leaf, 1 parsley sprig

1 large butternut squash (3 pounds or a little less)

4 plump garlic cloves

20 or so sage leaves or $1^{1}/_{2}$ tablespoons dried

packed $^{1}/_{2}$ cup parsley leaves

$^{1}/_{4}$ cup olive oil

1 large onion, cut into $^{1}/_{2}$-inch squares

1 cup lightly toasted walnuts or hazelnuts, finely chopped

sea salt and freshly ground pepper

$3^{1}/_{2}$ tablespoons butter

$3^{1}/_{2}$ tablespoons flour

1 8-ounce package no-boil lasagne noodles

1 cup grated Gruyère cheese

1 cup freshly grated Parmesan cheese

3 bunches of black kale, washed

pinch of hot red pepper flakes

1. Butter or oil a 9- by 12-inch baking dish. Preheat the oven to 375°F. In a small pot, slowly heat the milk with the aromatics. When it's nearly boiling, cover the pot, turn off the heat, and let it stand.

2. Peel the squash and chop it into a rough dice about ½-inch across or less. Chop 2 of the garlic cloves with the sage and parsley. Heat 2 tablespoons of the oil in a wide skillet or Dutch oven. Add the onion and squash and cook over high heat, stirring frequently, for about 15 minutes. Reduce the heat to medium and continue cooking, stirring occasionally, until the squash is fairly tender and caramelized in places, about 10 minutes. Add the garlic-herb mixture and the nuts. Cook for a few minutes longer, then turn off the heat. Season with salt and pepper to taste.

3. Melt the butter in a saucepan and stir in the flour. Reheat the milk and pour it through a strainer into the roux, whisking briskly. Turn the heat to low and cook, stirring occasionally, until the sauce thickens and the flour is cooked, 15 to 20 minutes. Season with ½ teaspoon salt and pepper to taste.

4. Spread ½ cup of the sauce in the baking dish and lay 3 noodles over it. Cover with half the squash mixture, 1 cup of the sauce, half the Gruyère, and a third of the Parmesan. Repeat, then add the third layer of noodles. Spread the remaining sauce over them, top with the remaining Parmesan and tent with foil. (At this point the lasagne can be held in the refrigerator until you're ready to bake it.) Bake for 30 minutes, then remove the foil and continue baking until bubbly and golden, 20 minutes longer. Remove from the oven and let rest while you cook the kale. (Lasagne, once well wrapped, can be frozen for up to a month. Before baking at 375°F, allow it to return to room temperature.)

5. Strip the kale leaves from their ropy stems and cut them into ½-inch strips. Heat the remaining oil in a skillet, add the rest of the garlic cloves, peeled and crushed, and cook long enough for it to perfume the oil and turn pale gold. Add the pepper flakes and the kale. Season with a few pinches of salt, toss in the pan to coat with the oil, then add 2 cups water. Lower the heat, cover the pan, and cook until the leaves are tender, 12 to 20 minutes, depending on their toughness. Don't undercook it. Taste for salt.

6. To serve, divide the kale among 6 plates and top each with a square of the lasagne.

Lasagne
with zucchini, ricotta, and tomato sauce

Make the tomato sauce first; you'll need it before you can assemble the lasagne.

Here's squash in lasagne once more, but this time it's summer squash. With this recipe, there will be no reason to complain about there being too much zucchini.

The quality of ricotta is very important—not just here but wherever ricotta is called for. I strongly recommend a whole-milk ricotta that has a smooth texture and sweet, delicate flavor. Many are grainy, especially the low-fat ones, so get to know what your stores offer and find a brand you like.

To make this a dairyless dish, replace the ricotta with 1 block well-drained firm or soft tofu, mashed and seasoned well with garlic, basil, salt, and pepper. Omit other cheeses.

You might start this summer supper with a contrasting bowl of fresh tomato soup or a salad of sliced layered tomatoes and quaff a crisp Pinot Blanc from Chalone Vineyard or a classic Sonoma Zinfandel such as Seghesio Home Ranch.

$2\frac{1}{2}$ cups tomato sauce (page 202 or 203)

1 pound ricotta cheese, preferably whole-milk

sea salt and freshly ground pepper

$2\frac{1}{2}$ pounds small zucchini

olive oil as needed

1 8-ounce package no-boil lasagne noodles

1 cup finely chopped walnuts or pine nuts

$\frac{1}{2}$ pound fresh mozzarella cheese (2 balls), grated or shredded

1 cup freshly grated Parmesan or pecorino cheese

1. Preheat the oven to 350°F. Lightly oil a 9- by 12-inch baking pan. Make the tomato sauce. It can be chunky or smooth, as you like. If the ricotta is densely textured, thin it with several tablespoons water and season with salt and pepper. If it's milky and wet, set it in a fine strainer to drain while you go on to the next step.

2. Cut the zucchini in half lengthwise. Cut each half into diagonal slices as thinly as possible. Heat the oil in large nonstick skillet. Add the zucchini and cook over medium-high heat, turning frequently, until it glistens and is tender, about 5 minutes.

3. Spread $\frac{1}{2}$ cup tomato sauce over the baking dish and set 3 noodles over it. Cover with a third of the ricotta, dot with a third of the nuts, and cover with a third of the zucchini. Season with salt and pepper, then cover with $\frac{1}{2}$ cup of the tomato sauce, a quarter of the mozzarella, and a sprinkling of Parmesan. Add the second layer of noodles

and repeat twice more. Cover the final layer of pasta with the remaining tomato sauce, mozzarella, and Parmesan.

4. Tent the dish with foil and bake until bubbling hot, about 40 minutes. Let rest for several minutes before serving.

Fideos
with pasilla chiles, avocado, and crema

SERVES 4

This *sopa seca,* or dry soup, from Mexico, made with the skinny, short noodles called *fideos,* is cooked pilaf style. The result is a soft noodle dish that is sort of an elaborate, spicy version of spaghetti with tomato sauce. Broiled or seared Roma tomatoes are my preference for the sauce, but in winter, a good season for this dish, Muir Glen's Fire-Roasted Tomatoes make an acceptable substitute. Eight ounces of noodles make reasonable portions for four adults, but two hungry teenagers can probably polish it off.

I would start this meal with a salad of watercress, pomegranates, and grapefruit, or grapefruit sections with romaine hearts and a lime vinaigretté. With the fideos, drink a Mexican beer or a dry sparkling wine, such as an Italian Prosecco. The sweet and spicy elements call for the scrape of bubbles.

First soften the dried chiles and roast the tomatoes for the sauce. Next brown the noodles, then cook them in the sauce. Add the garnishes and serve.

3 dried pasilla, New Mexican, or guajillo chiles

4 plump garlic cloves, unpeeled

3 tablespoons sunflower seed oil

8 Roma tomatoes or 1 15-ounce can Muir Glen Fire-Roasted Tomatoes, drained and juice reserved

sea salt and freshly ground pepper

$^{1}/_{2}$ cup chopped onion

$^{1}/_{2}$ pound short, skinny egg noodles (can be noodle nests or linguine or broken pieces)

3 parsley sprigs, plus a little coarsely chopped parsley to finish

$^{1}/_{2}$ cup Mexican crema, crème fraîche, or sour cream

a 2- to 3-ounce chunk feta cheese or queso fresco

1 avocado, peeled and sliced, for garnish

Pickled Onions for garnish (page 169)

pasta with vegetables

1. Cover the dried chiles with hot water and set them aside to soften while you make the tomato sauce. When soft, tear or cut the flesh into strips. Discard the seeds.

2. Moisten the unpeeled garlic cloves with a little of the oil, then cook them in a small skillet over medium-low heat, occasionally sliding the cloves around the pan, until the skins are toasted and the cloves are soft, 10 to 15 minutes. If using fresh tomatoes, coat them lightly with oil and grill over an open flame or on an *asador* (a Mexican stove-top grill) or sear them in a hot skillet to blister the skins. Squeeze the garlic from the skins into a blender and add the charred tomatoes, 1 teaspoon salt, the onion, and the reserved tomato juice plus water to make 1 cup. Puree.

3. Heat the remaining oil in a 10-inch cast-iron or nonstick skillet over medium-high heat. If the noodles are coiled or long, crumble them into pieces about 1½ inches in length. Add the noodles to the oil and stir them around until they're lightly browned, then add the tomato sauce and parsley. Add all but a few of the torn chiles, then even out the contents, and adjust the heat to a simmer. Cover the pan and cook until the noodles are soft, 15 to 20 minutes. Season with pepper.

4. Loosen the cream with a fork, then drizzle it over the surface of the finished dish. Crumble the cheese over the cream, scatter on the remaining chile pieces, and slice the avocado over all. Add a little chopped parsley and some pickled onions and serve, being sure to scrape up all the delectable crust that lurks on the bottom of the pan.

Lentils and Shells
with cilantro-scented onions, spinach,
and spinach crowns

Spinach crowns are the rosy base of each plant, including a few inches of the stems. They're usually thrown out, but they're delicious and very pretty.

If you use brown lentils and whole wheat pasta here, your dish will look, quite frankly, drab. Since we eat with our eyes, look for black or French green lentils instead of brown to make this dish as appealing to the eye as it is to the tongue. The lentils— sparked with spinach and onions seasoned with cumin, lime, and cilantro—snuggle right into the pasta shells. If you like them soupy, you can simply add a little of the lentil broth. This is an ideal dish to make when you have leftover lentils, pasta, or even cooked rice to use in place of or along with the pasta. Vegan, unless butter is used.

I'd start this supper with an appetizer of warm whole wheat flatbread or crackers, a garlicky yogurt cheese, some oil-cured olives, and something raw for brightness—cucumbers, cherry tomatoes, or sliced fennel. As for wine, a New World Syrah from Qupé in Santa Barbara has some fruit for the spice and some heartiness for the lentils.

1 cup green (Le Puy) or black (Beluga) lentils, rinsed	3 tablespoons olive oil or mixed olive oil and butter
herb bouquet: 1 bay leaf, 1 celery rib, and 2 thyme sprigs, tied together	2 large onions, sliced $1/4$ inch thick
sea salt and freshly ground pepper	1 scant cup chopped cilantro
1 bunch of spinach, the leaves cut at the stems, the base trimmed to include about 3 inches of the stems	$1/2$ teaspoon ground cumin or more to taste
	3 tablespoons chopped mint (optional)
	1 large lime, halved
	$1/2$ pound small pasta shells

1. Simmer the lentils in 6 cups water with the herb bouquet and $1/2$ teaspoon salt until very soft but not mushy, 35 minutes or so. Cover and let stand when finished. Bring a pot of water to a boil for the pasta.

2. While the lentils are cooking, slice off the spinach crowns, leaving about 3 inches of the stems. Pick off any roots and funky-looking parts, and set the crowns aside in a bowl of water to soak for at least 15 minutes. Discard the rest of the stems. Coarsely chop

the spinach leaves, then wash them well and set aside in a colander. Vigorously rinse the crowns to get rid of any sand.

3. Heat 2 tablespoons of the oil in a skillet over medium-high heat. Add the onions and cook, stirring frequently, until golden, about 20 minutes. Stir in the cilantro, cumin, and mint. Turn off the heat and squeeze the limes over the onions. Season well with salt and pepper.

4. When the pasta water boils, add salt and the pasta and cook until al dente. Scoop it out and add it to the lentils. Add the spinach to the pot, cook until just wilted, after several minutes, then add to the lentils and pasta. Blanch the crowns for 1 minute, then scoop them out.

5. Toss the lentils, pasta, and spinach with half the onions and a teaspoon of the remaining oil. Taste for salt and season with pepper. Spoon the remaining onions and spinach crowns over the top, drizzle the last of the oil over all, and serve.

- In summer, seed and dice 3 or 4 ripe tomatoes and toss them with fresh mint, cilantro, and a few pinches of salt, then spoon them over the lentils in place of or along with the onions.
- Serve with yogurt or a garlicky yogurt sauce.
- Cook extra lentils so that you have them on hand for a lentil salad later in the week.
- Instead of spinach, use collards, chard, or more aggressive greens, such as broccoli rabe, turnip greens, and mustard.
- If cilantro's not your herb, try dill (using a third as much) or a combination of dill, basil, and mint. Fresh marjoram and oregano are also good with lentils.
- Use the lentil-cooking water in a soup—it should be delicious.

Variations

Pasta and Chickpeas
with plenty of parsley and garlic

SERVES 4

This is one of the simplest dishes you can make. The pasta and chickpeas are tossed with a big lively bunch of parsley that's been chopped with lots of garlic and sage. For pasta, I like the organic whole wheat shells made by Bionaturae in Italy. Its flavor is not grimly "healthy," but it is robust enough to stand up to the chickpeas. There are lots of ways to play with this dish—see the variations—and it's vegan if you don't add the cheese.

A Primitivo from Puglia, or its cousin, a Zinfandel from Sonoma, would be a good wine to serve.

Start the water boiling for the pasta. Heat and season the chickpeas, cook the pasta, and put the two together.

1 tablespoon olive oil, plus extra to finish	3 plump garlic cloves
½ large onion, diced	small handful of sage leaves
a few pinches of hot red pepper flakes	sea salt and freshly ground pepper
1½ cups cooked chickpeas or 1 15-ounce can, preferably organic, liquid reserved	¾ pound whole wheat pasta shells freshly grated Parmesan
1 big bunch of flat-leaf parsley, the leaves stripped from the stems	

1. Bring a large pot of water to a boil for the pasta.

2. Heat the oil in a wide skillet and add the onion and pepper flakes. Cook for a few minutes, then add the chickpeas. While they're warming, chop the parsley, garlic, and sage together, then toss a third of it into the pan. Season well with salt and pepper, add a little water or chickpea broth to the pan, and cook slowly, adding more liquid as it cooks away.

3. Salt the pasta water and cook the pasta. When done, drain and toss it with the chickpeas, the rest of the parsley mixture, and extra olive oil to taste. Taste for salt and season with freshly ground pepper. Grate some cheese over the top and serve with additional pepper flakes.

Variations

• In summer, cut up a few garden tomatoes and add them at the very end.

• Enliven the dish with some grated lemon zest.

• Dark green (Le Puy) or black (Beluga) lentils are delicious here. If you have some cooked, add them to the chickpeas or use them in their stead.

• Mild ricotta or more pungent slivers of ricotta salata are both good in this pasta.

pasta with vegetables

Noodles
with a sauce of carrot tops, radish greens, and yogurt

This sauce is a bit mysterious because it's made from those greens that we usually discard—carrot tops and radish leaves—and whose flavor eludes us. They're lively, interesting, and tangy, especially when mixed with the yogurt. This dish is not meant to be served piping hot, because the yogurt will curdle if brought to a boil. But that makes it an especially appealing dish for hot weather. Vegans can omit the yogurt and toss the pasta with the pureed greens.

These unusual flavors can be met with the crisp acidity and lively fruit found in an unoaked Sauvignon Blanc. Try one from New Zealand's Marlborough region.

Variation In place of the feta and pine nuts, halve a pint of cherry tomatoes, toss them with minced chile, cilantro, and a little lime juice, and set them aside to come to room temperature while you make the dish. Spoon them over the pasta just before serving.

1 bunch of spinach (about 4 cups packed loose leaves)

tops from 1 or 2 bunches of carrots, the leaves stripped off the stems

leaves from 1 bunch of radishes

1 small bunch of cilantro, stems included, chopped (about 1 cup)

a handful of dill

4 lovage or celery leaves

1 cup whole-milk yogurt or sour cream

1 tablespoon olive oil

1 jalapeño chile, seeded and chopped

$\frac{1}{4}$ white onion, thinly sliced

sea salt

$\frac{3}{4}$ pound spaghetti or linguine

$\frac{1}{2}$ cup pine nuts

crumbled feta or Manouri cheese (optional)

1. Sort through the greens and discard any funky-looking leaves. Wash and chop them coarsely. Pour the yogurt into a fine-mesh strainer or cheesecloth to drain. Heat a large pot of salted water for the pasta.

2. Heat the oil in a wide nonstick skillet. Add the chile and onion and cook over medium heat, stirring occasionally, for a few minutes or until the onion turns translucent. Next add the greens with the water clinging to their leaves. Sprinkle with 1 teaspoon salt and cook until wilted, turning them with a pair of tongs after 3 or 4 minutes. Puree with the drained yogurt, then transfer the mixture to a large skillet. Turn the heat on low to warm the yogurt. Don't get it too hot or it will curdle.

3. Cook the pasta in the salted water until al dente, then drain. While it's cooking, toast the pine nuts in a small skillet until golden. Add the pasta to the sauce, toss well, and salt to taste. Scatter the cheese and pine nuts over the top.

Pasta
with eggplant, tomato, and ricotta salata

This summer pasta is one that I make at least once when eggplant and tomatoes are truly at their peak. To keep the eggplant from absorbing too much oil, I salt it for several hours beforehand. If you prefer, broil it as described in the eggplant gratin on page 24. When I have fresh cherry tomatoes in my garden, I dice a handful, toss them with some of the basil, then spoon them over the pasta just before serving. An excellent vegan pasta can be made without the cheese.

Serve this rich, summery pasta with a Sicilian rosé or white wine from Regaleali.

2 pounds eggplant, any variety	1 garlic clove, minced
sea salt and freshly ground pepper	12 basil leaves, slivered
$\frac{1}{2}$ pound Roma or other ripe plum-type tomatoes, peeled	a 3-ounce chunk of ricotta salata, thinly sliced
5 tablespoons olive oil	a handful of fresh tomatoes, diced and tossed with some of the basil
$\frac{3}{4}$ pound pasta wheels or spaghetti	
1 small onion, thinly sliced	Parmigiano-Reggianio for grating

1. Peel the eggplant and cut it into pieces about $1\frac{1}{2}$ inches long and $\frac{1}{2}$ inch wide. Toss with a teaspoon of salt and set aside for several hours. When you're ready to cook, rinse off the salt, then squeeze it in an absorbent towel to wick off the water.

2. Slice the peeled tomatoes lengthwise into quarters, pull out the seeds, then cut them into strips. If you're not using them for a while, toss the strips in a little olive oil.

3. Put on a big pot of water for the pasta. Heat a large skillet with $\frac{1}{4}$ cup oil. When hot (a piece of eggplant should sizzle when you drop it in), add the eggplant and quickly give it a stir. Cook over high heat, stirring frequently, lowering the heat if the pan seems too hot, until the eggplant is browned and tender, 12 to 15 minutes. Turn it onto paper towels and wipe out the pan. Salt the boiling water and add the pasta.

4. Return the pan to the stove and reduce the heat since it will already be very hot. Add a tablespoon of oil, then the onion, and cook for several minutes until it's pale gold and soft. Add the garlic and the tomato strips. Cook for several minutes, then add the eggplant to the pan and the basil, along with a little pasta water.

5. When the pasta is done, add it to the pan and toss with the ricotta salata. Serve, garnished with the fresh tomatoes, pepper, and a dusting of freshly grated cheese.

Cut and salt the eggplant and set aside for 3 or more hours, then rinse and blot it dry. You can peel and slice the sauce tomatoes early on, too, toss them with a little oil, and set aside until needed. The sauce and pasta cook pretty much simultaneously. Peel the tomatoes with a paring knife or by dipping them for 10 seconds or so into boiling water and then slipping off the skins.

pasta with vegetables

Labor Day Spaghetti
with golden peppers, black olives,
and sun gold tomatoes

Cook the peppers and onions while the water is coming to a boil. Then cook the pasta and combine with the uncooked tomatoes.

It's not until around Labor Day that the sweet, thick-fleshed golden bell peppers are finally ready. This pasta is one way to celebrate them, along with the end of the summer. The little tomatoes, which are left whole, explode in your mouth. If you peel the peppers with a vegetable peeler, they'll get a silky texture and leave no unpleasant scrolls of skin. Peppers with nice flat sides are the easiest ones to peel. This pasta is vegan as is, but I would follow it with a selection of goat cheeses and white nectarines for dessert.

A crisp, chilled white that is also a little fruity—a Sauvignon Blanc, Pinot Blanc, or Chenin Blanc—would support this robust late-summer dish.

sea salt and freshly ground pepper

¾ pound spaghetti

2 tablespoons olive oil, plus extra to finish

4 to 5 golden bell peppers, peeled and cut lengthwise into ½-inch strips

1 red onion, thinly sliced

2 garlic cloves, finely chopped

½ cup dry white wine

½ cup chopped black olives

3 tablespoons salt capers, rinsed and soaked (see page 214)

⅔ cup chopped parsley

2 cups Sun Gold or other bite-sized tomatoes, left whole

1. Bring a pot of water to boil for the spaghetti. When it boils, add plenty of salt and the pasta, then cook until al dente.

2. Heat the oil in a wide, deep pan such as a Dutch oven. Add the peppers and onion and cook over high heat, tossing them about the pan to sear them. After 4 or 5 minutes, add the garlic, pour in the wine, and deglaze the pan, scraping up the pan juices. Lower the heat to medium and add the olives, capers, half the parsley, and a scoop of water from the pasta pot. Season with salt and plenty of pepper. Add the little tomatoes, simmer for a minute, then turn off the heat.

3. When the spaghetti is done, drain, then toss it with olive oil to taste. Divide among warm serving bowls, spoon the peppers and tomatoes over each, garnish with the remaining parsley, and serve.

crêpes and fritters

*t*riangles, half-moons, ovals, and stacks are simple, friendly, and amusing forms. Crêpes and fritterlike things have such shapes, which focus the eye on what's for supper. If these homey little dishes sound old-fashioned, know that crêpes never really go out of style. If you're worried about deep-frying, rest assured that neither the skillet cakes nor the fritters are deep-fried. Of course, that means that the latter aren't true fritters, but I can't think of a better name for crispy sautéed cakes and morsels.

Quick, economical, and versatile crêpes make a great companion for vegetable stews and braises and a fine wrapper for vegetables like asparagus. But you needn't limit yourself to folding or rolling them. Flop a crêpe on a plate, cover it with its filling, and lay a second one over the top, and even that's enough to transform a mélange of vegetables into a focused main dish. You can make a stack of crêpes and their fillings, then slice them into wedges, and you can even pour your batter over the vegetables and bake the whole thing.

Sautéed disks of grated vegetables bound with egg, seasoned with herbs, then crisped in olive oil are what I refer to as *skillet cakes,* whereas fritters and croquettes, based more on grain than on vegetables, are plump little units with crisp, crunchy exteriors. All lend themselves to accompaniments of sauces and toppings of vegetable salads. And while they aren't meant to be fake meatballs or hamburgers, the Brown Rice–Mushroom "Burgers" (page 84) and Feather Fritters (page 85) can, with their earthy flavors and chewy textures, effectively stand in for ground meat in such dishes as the Cabbage Parcels on page 157.

4

Spinach Crêpe Cake
with herbed ricotta and mushrooms

Because the spinach goes right into the batter, these crêpes are green throughout, a bit thicker than normal, and a little spongy. While you can certainly fold or roll them, I like to layer the crêpes with the ricotta, then smother them with the sautéed mushrooms.

You might start this supper with a soup such as carrot soup with the carrot greens and conclude with a simple green salad. For wine, you could serve a nicely oaked Chardonnay from Domaine Serene or a sparkling wine such as Tony Soter's, both from Oregon.

THE CRÊPES

1 bunch of spinach, stems removed and leaves well washed but not dried,
  or about 1 cup cooked frozen spinach

sea salt

1½ cups milk

3 eggs

3 tablespoons melted butter, olive oil, or sunflower seed oil, plus extra for the pan

1 tablespoon chopped marjoram or tarragon

1 cup all-purpose flour

THE RICOTTA FILLING

2 cups ricotta cheese, preferably whole-milk

1 cup freshly grated Parmesan cheese

2 tablespoons chopped parsley

1 tablespoon chopped marjoram or tarragon

1 tablespoon snipped chives or finely minced scallion

sea salt

THE MUSHROOMS

2 tablespoons butter, olive oil, or a mixture

3 scallions or 1 shallot, finely chopped

1 pound mushrooms, one or several varieties, sliced about ¼ inch thick

freshly ground pepper

½ cup dry white wine

1 tablespoon chopped parsley, marjoram, or tarragon

½ cup cream, mushroom broth, and/or light cream or crème fraîche

1. If using fresh, drop the wet spinach into a wide skillet, sprinkle with salt, and cook for a few minutes until wilted. Put the cooked spinach in a food processor with the milk, eggs, butter, and herb and pulse a few times to puree. Add the flour and 1 teaspoon salt, then puree until smooth. Set aside to rest for at least 20 minutes while you season the ricotta and prep the mushrooms.

2. Heat a little butter or oil in an 8-inch skillet. Give the batter a stir, then pour in $1/4$ to $1/3$ cup and swirl it around the pan. Cook over medium heat until set and golden on the bottom, 2 to 3 minutes. Pry up the edges, turn the crêpe over with your fingers, and briefly cook the other side until it becomes dry enough to slide in the pan, about 30 seconds. The second side will be bright green. Add a little fat each time you make a crêpe as they tend to stick a little.

3. Mix all the ingredients for the ricotta filling together and season to taste with salt.

4. Using 3 crêpes per person, spread 2 tablespoons of the ricotta over one, cover with a second crêpe, repeat with the ricotta, and cover with the third crêpe, the greenest side facing up. If you have two skillets that will accommodate the stacks, melt a little butter or oil them, add the stacked crêpes, cover the pan, and cook over medium-low heat until heated through, about 12 minutes. Otherwise, place them on a sheet pan, cover with foil, and bake at 375°F until heated through, 15 to 20 minutes.

5. While the crêpes are heating, cook the mushrooms: Melt the butter in a large skillet. Add the scallions and cook over medium heat for a minute, then raise the heat and add the mushrooms. Season with salt and pepper and cook, tossing frequently, until they begin to color. Add the wine and let it reduce. When the mushrooms are tender, add the herb and the cream or mushroom broth. Taste for salt and season with pepper. Don't let the liquid cook away—you'll want a little sauce.

6. Place a crêpe stack on each plate, spoon the mushrooms and their juices over them, and serve.

Masa Crêpes
with chard, chiles, and cilantro

Make the crêpe batter
first so that it can rest
while you cook the
chard, heat the beans,
and make the salsa.
Then cook the crêpes
and fill them.

This started out as a Mexican *budin,* a casserole so dense with tortillas, sour cream, and cheese that in the end it was simply too rich, even for me. But as I love the flavors of the various elements, I put them into these lighter corn crêpes and, if supper is very informal, I let each person fill his or her own. Otherwise, I fill them and heat them in a skillet or the oven. For a vegan version, use corn tortillas in place of the crêpes and nondairy cheeses.

Serve these crêpes with black beans (page 208), a dollop of sour cream, and something fresh, such as slivered jícama and cucumbers with lime and chile. An unoaked wine such as Domaine Chandon's sparkling wine or a slightly chilled Beaujolais would make a refreshing, informal match for these crêpes.

THE CRÊPES

3 eggs

$1^{1}/_{2}$ cups milk

$^{1}/_{2}$ cup masa harina, roasted corn flour, or fine cornmeal

$^{1}/_{2}$ cup flour

$^{1}/_{2}$ teaspoon sea salt

3 tablespoons melted butter or oil

THE CHARD FILLING

$1^{1}/_{2}$ tablespoons light olive oil

1 large white onion, finely diced

1 or 2 jalapeño chiles, finely diced, seeds removed if you don't want their heat

$1^{1}/_{2}$ teaspoons dried Mexican oregano

2 garlic cloves, minced

1 heaping cup cilantro, chopped

2 or even 3 big bunches of chard, any color, stems removed, leaves roughly chopped

sea salt

$^{1}/_{3}$ cup sour cream, plus extra for serving

1 cup grated cheese, such as Oaxacan string cheese, queso blanco, Jack, or Muenster

1. Put all the ingredients for the crêpes in a blender and blend until smooth, scraping down the sides once or twice as needed. Pour into a liquid measuring cup and set aside.

2. Heat the oil in a large nonstick skillet. Add the onion, chiles, and oregano and cook over medium heat, stirring occasionally, until softened, 6 to 8 minutes. Add the garlic and cilantro and cook for a few minutes more, then add the chard and cook, turning the leaves occasionally until wilted. Season with salt to taste, and cook until the chard is tender, 4 to 5 minutes. Stir in the sour cream.

3. Cook the crêpes in an 8-inch skillet, stacking them up on a plate as you go so that they hold their heat. You should end up with about 10 crêpes. With the prettier side facing down, spread half the crêpe with the chard, add a little cheese, then fold them in half and again into quarters.

4. To reheat in a skillet, film it lightly with oil over medium-high heat and add the crêpes. Cook on both sides, the pan covered, until heated through, then serve.

SERVES 4 # Buckwheat Crêpes
with fried eggs

If you've made your crêpes ahead of time, all you have to do is fold and heat them, cook your eggs, and then bring them together. If you're making the batter at the last minute, it needn't rest before cooking because there's relatively little gluten in it.

Three flecked buckwheat crêpes folded over Gruyère cheese and topped with a fried egg make a supper that's special yet not difficult. Even if you haven't any previously cooked crêpes on hand, you can still pull this off at the last minute since the batter is a quick one-two-three sort of operation. (I've also used the buckwheat pancake mix from Bob's Red Mill—just make it thinner than the instructions call for.

You might serve these crêpes with a chopped apple and celery or celery root salad and for dessert a compote of pears, persimmons, and figs. To drink, try hard apple cider or a crisp Sancerre from the Loire Valley.

¾ cup water

¾ cup milk

3 eggs

½ cup buckwheat flour

¾ cup all-purpose flour

¾ teaspoon sea salt

½ teaspoon sugar

3 tablespoons melted butter or sunflower seed oil, plus extra for the pan

grated Gruyère cheese

butter for the pan

1 or 2 eggs per person

sea salt and freshly ground pepper

1. Put all the crêpe ingredients in a blender jar and blend until smooth, stopping after 30 seconds or so to scrape down the sides of the jar.

2. Heat an 8-inch nonstick skillet or crêpe pan, wipe a little butter over the surface, then add about ¼ cup batter and swirl it around the pan. Cook over medium heat until you can loosen the edge of the crêpe and pick it up with your fingers, about 2 minutes. Then turn it over and cook the second side just until it no longer sticks. Slide the crêpe out onto a plate and continue, stacking them up as you go.

3. With the pretty side of each crêpe facing down, grate a little cheese over the surface, then fold loosely into quarters. Melt a little butter in a large nonstick skillet and add the crêpes, allowing 3 per person. Cook on both sides, over medium heat, until hot and slightly crisp around the edges.

4. Melt another bit of butter in a nonstick skillet. Break in the eggs, season with salt and pepper, and cook them as you like them—sunny side up or turned, wet or dry. Or poach the eggs if you prefer.

5. Arrange 3 crêpes on each plate, lay the egg in the middle, add a little cracked pepper, and serve.

Shredded Root Vegetable Ragout
under a wild rice pancake

The rice can be cooked days in advance, and the vegetables can be cooked a few hours ahead of time if that's convenient. If you're going from zero to the table, make the pancake batter first so that it can rest, but wait until the last minute to add the egg whites. Cook the vegetables, cover them with the batter, and put them right in the oven.

Here the rice-studded batter is poured over the ragout, then baked, making a savory cakelike topping. However, there's no reason you can't make the batter into crêpes, flop one on the plate and another over the vegetables, then serve with sour cream or the goat cheese sauce on page 201. For a vegan version, simply serve the ragout with wild rice.

A German or Alsatian Riesling would be a crisp, lively beverage to swirl and sip with this dish.

THE WILD RICE PANCAKES

2 cups cooked wild rice or long-grain brown rice

3 eggs, separated

1 cup milk

3 tablespoons oil or melted butter

¾ cup whole wheat pastry flour or all-purpose flour

2 teaspoons baking powder

sea salt and freshly ground pepper

2 scallions, including some of the greens, thinly sliced

1 tablespoon chopped tarragon

1 tablespoon chopped parsley

THE RAGOUT

2 tablespoons olive oil

2 bay leaves

1 red onion, finely diced

2 tablespoons chopped tarragon

1 large red beet, peeled and coarsely grated

1 large carrot, peeled and coarsely grated

1 large parsnip, peeled and coarsely grated

4 cups thinly sliced red cabbage

sea salt and freshly ground pepper

1 tart apple, grated

1 tablespoon tomato paste

¹⁄₂ cup vinegar: apple-balsamic, balsamic, or aged red wine

¹⁄₂ cup toasted walnuts, chopped

5 ounces fresh goat cheese

sour cream for serving

1. Oil a 9- by 12-inch gratin dish or 6 large individual gratin dishes.

2. Chop half the wild rice finely and leave the rest whole. Mix the egg yolks with the milk and oil, then whisk in the flour, baking powder, ¹⁄₂ teaspoon salt, and the rice. Stir in the scallions and herbs and season with pepper. Let the batter rest while you prepare the vegetables.

3. Heat the oil in a wide skillet with the bay leaves. Add the onion and tarragon, sauté over medium-high heat for a few minutes, then add the beet, carrot, parsnip, and cabbage. Season with 1 teaspoon salt and cook, frequently turning the vegetables in the pan, until the cabbage is tender, 10 minutes or longer. Halfway through the cooking, add the apple and ¹⁄₂ cup water so that the vegetables stay moist.

4. Once the vegetables are tender, stir in the tomato paste and vinegar. Toss well, taste for salt, season with pepper, then turn off the heat. If no moisture remains, add another ¹⁄₂ cup water. Stir in the nuts, then transfer the vegetables to the prepared baking dish(es). Cover and refrigerate if you're not ready to finish the dish at this point. Otherwise, preheat the oven to 375°F.

5. When ready to bake, crumble the goat cheese into the vegetables and toss briefly. Whip the egg whites with a pinch of salt until stiff, then fold them into the batter. Give a turn before pouring it over the vegetables so that the rice is distributed evenly. Bake until puffed and heated through, about 25 minutes. Serve with sour cream on the side.

Zucchini Skillet Cakes
with capers and pine nuts

These versatile skillet cakes take well to all kinds of herbal seasonings, but I especially like this combination of marjoram with capers, pine nuts, and a bit of lemon. They can be served naked, topped with a little salad of cherry tomatoes, or accompanied with a creamy ranch dressing. To make these skillet cakes vegan, replace the eggs with pureed tofu.

These are not particularly dense, so include something more substantial in your meal if appetites are large. A rice pilaf or quinoa and a big salad with lots of vegetables would do the trick. To drink, a crisp white wine, such as a Russian River Sauvignon Blanc—Rochioli, for example—would have the acidity to stand up to the capers, with enough fruit to wrap around the zucchini.

4 cups grated zucchini (from about 2 pounds or 6 medium squash)

sea salt and freshly ground pepper

2 eggs, beaten, or ½ cup pureed tofu

3 tablespoons snipped chives

1 garlic clove, minced or pounded in a mortar

½ cup chopped parsley

3 tablespoons chopped marjoram or 2 teaspoons dried

grated zest of 1 lemon

1 cup dried bread crumbs

½ cup pine nuts, lightly toasted in a dry skillet

¼ cup capers, rinsed

olive oil for frying

1. Toss the grated zucchini with a teaspoon of salt and set it aside in a colander while you prepare the rest of the ingredients. Then rinse the zucchini and squeeze out as much moisture as you can.

2. Toss the zucchini with the eggs, chives, garlic, parsley, marjoram, and lemon zest. Stir in the bread crumbs along with the pine nuts and capers. To check the seasonings, fry a dab of the mixture, then taste it for salt and pepper and season the batter accordingly.

3. Film 2 large skillets with olive oil. When hot, add the batter in ½-cup measures. Spread the batter out a bit and cook over medium heat until golden. (Or make a single 6-inch skillet cake per person.) Turn and cook the second side. Serve right away or keep warm in the oven until all are done.

Brown Rice–Mushroom "Burgers"

If you haven't a cup of leftover rice or bulgur, make it first. Then cook the onion-mushroom-nut mixture. Put everything together in a food processor and pulse to a meatlike texture.

I am not a fan of faux burgers or other faux meat dishes, but when a friend insisted that we try her sister's recipe for a nut loaf at Greens restaurant in San Francisco, I was surprised at how tasty it was. And no wonder! It was loaded with cups of cashews and walnuts, more than $\frac{1}{2}$ pound of cheese, numerous eggs, and even cottage cheese. Nonetheless, the nut loaf proved to be such a versatile and popular dish on our menu that I've long wanted to make a modified version that's more suited to how we eat today. Here it is. It's hardly noncaloric, but it's vastly improved over the original and designed to be made into "veggie burgers," which you can serve with sautéed onions, mustard, and tomato. (You can also use it to stuff the cabbage leaves on page 157.) For nuts, I find that a combination of cashews and pecans or walnuts is best. You can make this a day or two ahead of time and refrigerate it before finishing. It's vegan if you use soy cheese and replace the egg with $\frac{1}{3}$ cup mashed tofu.

1 tablespoon olive oil or sunflower seed oil

1 large onion, diced

1 teaspoon crumbled dried sage leaves

2 pinches of dried thyme

$\frac{1}{2}$ pound mushrooms, chopped

$\frac{1}{2}$ cup cashews, roughly chopped

$\frac{1}{2}$ cup pecans, roughly chopped

1 teaspoon tamari or soy sauce or to taste

sea salt and freshly ground pepper

1 cup cooked brown rice or bulgur

$\frac{1}{2}$ cup grated Cheddar cheese

1 egg or $\frac{1}{3}$ cup drained mashed tofu

$\frac{1}{2}$ cup bread crumbs

1. Heat the oil in a medium skillet. Add the onion, crumble in the herbs, and cook over high heat, stirring frequently, until the onion is seared in places and starting to soften, 3 to 4 minutes. Add the mushrooms and nuts and cook, stirring frequently, until the mushrooms have released and then reabsorbed their juices, after several minutes. Stir in the tamari and season with $\frac{1}{2}$ teaspoon salt and pepper to taste.

2. Transfer this mixture to your food processor, add the rice, cheese, egg, and bread crumbs, and pulse so that the mixture resembles ground meat. Fry a dab in some olive oil to check the seasonings and correct if needed.

3. To cook, film a wide nonstick skillet with oil. Scoop out $\frac{1}{2}$-cup measures, then add them to the skillet and press down on them with a spatula so that the patties are about $\frac{1}{2}$ inch thick. Fry over medium heat until brown, 4 to 5 minutes, then turn and finish cooking the second side, another 4 minutes or so.

Feather Fritters

with squash "spaghetti" and tomato sauce

If I called these "meatless meatballs," they would sound so earnestly vegetarian that you'd probably pass right over them. But this is exactly what they are—airy bread-based morsels that derive from the *cucina povera* of Italy. I've had them in Puglia as appetizers—large, light, and deep-fried—but here I've made smaller spheres into a main dish, which includes a tomato sauce and spaghetti-like strands of winter squash. A wonderful rakelike tool made by Kuhn Rikon enables you to pull strands of squash off any of the delicious varieties of winter squash by dragging it over the peeled, uncooked flesh. If you don't have one of these gadgets, be sure to use spaghetti squash, which you can pull into strands with a fork.

You have to play with your ingredients to end up with a mixture that can be molded loosely into a ball. Bread that's bone dry will absorb a lot more milk than fresher bread. What's important is to use bread that has a strong crumb, or your fritters will be mushy. As for the tomato sauce, it can be either the quick or the long-simmered variety (page 202 or 203), both made from fresh tomatoes. If fresh is out of the question, know that you can also make a pretty good last-minute sauce using canned tomatoes, as here.

Pureed squash, actual spaghetti squash, and greens also make good accompaniments to these flavor-filled spheres. To drink, stay in the region and have Primitivo or go to Sonoma for a Zinfandel.

While the bread is soaking, prepare the rest of the ingredients. The actual cooking of the fritters, squash, and tomato sauce can happen later, when you're ready for them. The fritter mixture freezes well and can be a very convenient item to have on hand.

4 thick slices stale country bread, about $\frac{1}{2}$ pound with the crusts removed

$\frac{1}{2}$ to 1 cup milk or more as needed

2 tablespoons chopped marjoram or oregano

3 tablespoons chopped parsley

1 garlic clove

1 cup ricotta cheese

1 cup freshly grated Parmesan cheese

$\frac{1}{3}$ cup finely diced onion or shallot

1 or 2 eggs, as needed

sea salt and freshly ground pepper

olive oil for frying

8 cups winter squash strands

Five-Minute Tomato Sauce (page 204)

minced parsley or oregano for garnish

crêpes and fritters

1. Put the bread in a pie plate and pour the milk over it. If it's on the soft side, use little milk; if it's hard, use more. While you're chopping everything else, return to the bread now and then and move it around, squeezing the wet pieces over the drier ones. When all the bread is soft, squeeze out the excess milk. Put it in a food processor and pulse just enough to break it up into coarse crumbs, then turn it into a bowl.

2. Chop the herbs with the garlic and add them to the bread along with the cheeses, onion, and 1 egg. Season with 1 teaspoon salt and plenty of pepper. Mix everything together—your hands are the best tool—then fry a little batter in some olive oil until golden and taste it for salt. You'll also be able to tell if it's too dry (add another egg) or too wet (add more dried bread crumbs). Shape the dough into spheres or ovals, using about 2 teaspoons for each.

3. Film a cast-iron or nonstick skillet with olive oil. When hot, add the morsels, taking care not to crowd them, and cook over medium heat, shuffling the pan frequently so that all the surfaces brown.

4. Just before serving, drop the squash strands into boiling salted water and cook until tender, 3 to 5 minutes. Strain, then toss the strands with a little butter or olive oil and season with salt and pepper.

5. To serve, nap each plate with tomato sauce, heap the "spaghetti" over it, add the fritters, and garnish with a little minced parsley.

Lemony Risotto Croquettes
with slivered snow peas, asparagus, and leeks

The rice has to be cool before you can form it. While it's cooling, sliver the vegetables or prepare another part of the meal. You can keep the finished croquettes in a warm oven while you sauté the vegetables, but they take less than 5 minutes to cook.

I love risotto, but not as a main dish, unless something has been done to it to give it form. Here, a lemony risotto is formed into ovals, then shallow-fried until golden and crisp and served over a bed of finely slivered spring vegetables. These croquettes make a lovely supper dish for company and can be made vegan if no butter and eggs are used, although the egg does help bind the rice.

The vegetables needn't be these amounts. Work with what you have and what pleases you, just as long as everything is thinly sliced. Certainly include fresh English peas or fava beans if you can.

This rice isn't cooked with incremental additions of stock as it is for risotto, but in water and all at once. However, there's no reason not to use leftover risotto for croquettes and fritters. I can easily imagine red wine risotto croquettes with sautéed mushrooms, a summer squash risotto with a tomato concassé, and so forth. A croquette does not, in the end, make a heavy dish, so I'd start this spring meal with a creamy mushroom soup in contrast to the texture of the vegetables, add a salad of spring greens and herbs, and end with a rhubarb tart for dessert. A crisp, unoaked Arneis from the Piedmont, such as the Giacosa Arneis, would echo the citrus notes and encompass the vegetables.

THE RICE

1 tablespoon butter

3 bunches of scallions, including a few inches of the greens, thinly sliced

2 cups risotto rice, such as Arborio

sea salt and freshly ground pepper

finely grated zest of 2 lemons

2 tablespoons finely chopped parsley or basil

1 ball ($^1/_4$ pound) fresh mozzarella cheese, diced

$^1/_2$ cup freshly grated Parmesan cheese

3 eggs

3 cups bread crumbs

olive oil for frying

vegetarian suppers

3 tablespoons butter

2 fat leeks, white parts only, halved, cut into 2-inch pieces, and finely slivered

1 pound asparagus, tough ends snapped off, peeled if thick, then slivered, including the tips

2 big handfuls of snow peas, thinly slivered

2 handfuls of edible-pod peas, slivered

sea salt

2 tablespoons fresh lemon juice

2 teaspoons minced parsley, basil, or chervil

1. Bring 1 quart water to a simmer in a 3-quart pan with a tight-fitting lid. Melt the butter in a 10-inch skillet or sauté pan over medium-high heat. When sizzling, add the scallions. Cook, stirring frequently, for about 1 minute, then add the rice, turn to coat it with the butter, and cook for a minute or two. Stir in ½ teaspoon salt. Add the rice to the simmering water. Cover and cook over low heat for 16 minutes. Remove the lid, and if there's still water present, cook it off. Otherwise, stir in the lemon zest, parsley, pepper, and cheeses, then allow the rice to cool in the pan. Stir in one of the eggs.

2. Using a ⅓-cup measure, scoop out the rice and shape it to make an oval croquette.

3. Whisk the remaining eggs in a pie pan. Put the bread crumbs on another pie pan or plate. Using your left hand, dip each croquette into the egg mixture, then, using your right hand, gently roll it in the crumbs to coat. Set it aside on a tray covered with wax paper until all are made. (These can be refrigerated hours ahead of time, then brought back to room temperature before frying.)

4. When ready to eat, preheat the oven to 300°F if you're planning to hold them. Generously coat 2 wide skillets with olive oil. When hot, add the croquettes and cook over medium heat, gently turning them to brown them all over, 5 to 7 minutes total. Transfer them to a plate and set in the oven while you sauté the vegetables.

5. Heat half the butter until foaming in a wide sauté pan. Add all the slivered vegetables, sprinkle them with sea salt, and sauté over high heat for about 1½ minutes. Add the lemon juice and remaining butter, shuffling the pan over the heat so that they combine into a sauce. Add the herbs.

6. To serve, divide the vegetables among warm plates, then arrange the fritters attractively on top, allowing 3 per serving.

Sweet Souffléd Ricotta Cakes

We like pancakes not only for breakfast but for supper too on occasion. Pillowy and light, these golden cakes are delicious with dabs of sour cream and a favorite conserve. I don't sweeten the batter—it doesn't seem necessary—but add a teaspoon of sugar if you like. Easy to double if you're serving more than three people.

Serve with your favorite breakfast condiments, such as sour cream, raspberry jam or apricot preserves, warm maple syrup, or homemade applesauce. A glass of New Mexico's Gruet sparkling wine seems like a perfect drink to me to have with these little pancakes.

1 cup ricotta cheese	$1/2$ cup flour
3 eggs, separated	$1/4$ teaspoon sea salt
$1/2$ cup milk	1 teaspoon vanilla extract
3 tablespoons butter, melted in a wide	freshly grated nutmeg
nonstick skillet	

1. Beat the ricotta with the egg yolks until smooth, then stir in the milk and melted butter, followed by the flour and salt. Stir to make a smooth batter. Add the vanilla and grate a little nutmeg into the batter.

2. Whisk the egg whites until they form barely firm peaks, then fold them into the batter.

3. Reheat the skillet in which you melted the butter, then drop in the batter in $1/4$-cup dollops. Cook over medium heat until set and golden on the bottom and dimpled with holes on the top, about 3 minutes, then turn and cook the second side, without patting it down, another 2 minutes.

mostly tofu (and some tempeh)

*l*ike eggs, tofu and tempeh are not only good sources of protein but can provide you with a main dish literally within minutes. All the recipes in this chapter are vegan. Except for one, none require pressing the tofu before using it, and rather than being fried in oil, the tofu firms up and browns in its own oils in a dry skillet. You do need a good nonstick or seasoned cast-iron skillet to do this, however.

I have a special fondness for tofu and tempeh cooked with Asian flavors, so most of these recipes call for a number of Asian ingredients. Here's a brief glossary.

tofu: Unless specified organic, tofu is most likely made from genetically modified soybeans. Fortunately organic brands aren't hard to find. Even my supermarket carries them on a regular basis. I prefer tofu that's packed in water rather than in aseptic cartons—it's fresher and more flavorful. I use firm tofu if it's going to be sautéed, soft if it's going to braised. Usually a carton of tofu weighs around a pound, depending on the brand, which is enough for about three servings.

tempeh: Denser than tofu, tempeh is a live food made from fermented soybeans alone or mixed with other grains. It comes in blocks and is naturally flecked with dark spots. I find it more likable if I steam or simmer it first in a marinade, then brown it in a little oil before adding it to a dish. Like tofu, tempeh is easy to use and a quick source of protein.

soy sauce: When it comes to soy sauce, I am partial to San-J soy, a naturally brewed, full-bodied soy sauce, available at natural food stores. You'll probably have to go to an Asian market for dark, syrupy mushroom soy sauce. It has somewhat molassesy undertones, so use it in small amounts and gradually when adding it to a dish. Tamari is similar to soy sauce but richer and with a more pronounced, concentrated flavor. You can always taste it in a dish, so again, use it judiciously unless that's the flavor you want.

coconut milk: Regular coconut milk has a layer of coconut cream on top the light version doesn't. Cans vary in weight but are around 15 ounces. Just use the whole can regardless of the weight.

condiments: Black rice vinegar is dark, sweet, and rich, not dissimilar to balsamic vinegar, which can be used in its place. Lan Chi chili pastes add fire and robustness to a stir-fry. Thai chile pastes, now easily found at supermarkets and natural food stores, make a coconut milk–based curry pretty much an instant dish. I use them, because I can't always find kaffir lime leaves and lemon grass to make a paste from scratch. I also buy frozen minced lemon grass at Asian markets which isn't as good as fresh but is better than none.

I also consider roasted peanut oil and dark (roasted) sesame oil condiments. When added to a stir-fry or braise, they contribute a huge wallop of flavor. (For the initial sautéing I use light peanut or sesame oil.) Loriva brand roasted peanut oil is available at many supermarkets and specialty stores. I've been recommending it for almost twenty years! Unscrew the cap and inhale the aroma of roasting peanuts.

Skillet-Seared Tofu
with two sauces

This recipe may be familiar to those readers who have my book *This Can't Be Tofu!* but I include it here because with this technique you'll never have an excuse for not cooking dinner. It takes about ten minutes to go from the carton to the plate—scarcely time enough to get a salad or a side dish together.

This basic tofu is delicious alone and with the following two sauces, but you have a host of other options as well. You can smother it with sautéed mushrooms or onions, you can put it in a sandwich with the works, and you can even slice it thinly and then toss it with skinny udon noodles and the Peanut Sauce on page 200. There are endless possibilities—and all of them are vegan.

1 carton firm tofu packed in water, drained

2 teaspoons olive oil or vegetable oil

sea salt and freshly ground pepper

several dashes Worcestershire, steak, tamari, soy, or other sauce

slivered scallions and thin red bell pepper strips

1. Slice the tofu crosswise into 6 pieces and blot it with paper towels.

2. Heat the oil in a cast-iron or nonstick skillet. Add the tofu, sprinkle with salt, and cook over medium-high heat until golden. At first it will twitch around as the water in the tofu turns to steam, but then it will settle down. Once the first side is browned, turn and cook the second side, about 10 minutes in all. Shake on a tablespoon or two of the sauce and continue cooking until it evaporates, leaving the tofu seasoned and glazed. Season with pepper, scatter the scallions and peppers over all, and serve.

Miso Topping

You don't have to deglaze the tofu to use this topping, but I do. I like this version with brown rice (the sauce is good on it, too) and a slaw of slivered napa cabbage tossed with lime juice and a few drops of toasted sesame oil. An Alsatian Pinot Blanc would be an interesting match with the miso.

*mostly tofu
(and some tempeh)*

⅓ cup white (shiro) miso	several good grinds from the peppermill
2 tablespoons mirin	1 teaspoon roasted sesame oil
2 teaspoons grated fresh ginger	a small splash of soy sauce, to taste
1 plump garlic clove, minced or pressed	3 tablespoons mayonnaise

1. Preheat the broiler. Mix everything for the sauce together by hand or in a food processor until smooth.

2. Once you've seared your tofu, set the pieces on a pan, spread a mound of sauce over each piece, then broil until blistered, after a few minutes. Serve with an additional dab of sauce on each.

Tomato and Thai Basil Relish

Another way to serve your skillet tofu is to cover it with this summery tomato relish and drink a fruity Pinot Noir from Santa Barbara.

2 medium tomatoes or a big handful of smaller ones (about 2 cups)	1 teaspoon roasted peanut or sesame oil
1 small shallot or a few scallions, with an inch of greens, minced	juice and grated zest of 1 lime
	2 teaspoons freshly grated ginger
a small handful of Thai or Italian basil leaves	1 garlic clove, minced
a dozen small mint leaves, slivered	sea salt
	a small splash of soy sauce, to taste

Halve the tomatoes and remove the seeds if using large ones, then dice them into smallish pieces. If using an assortment of smaller ones, just slice them into halves or quarters and put them in a bowl. Add the rest of the ingredients and toss them together with a few pinches of salt. Let stand while you prepare the tofu. Deglaze with soy sauce, then serve with the relish spooned on top.

Brown Rice Supper
with tofu, roasted peanut sauce, and stir-fried carrots

The rice takes the longest, so start it first. Then go to the carrots, the sauce, and the tofu. Dinner will be done when the rice is. The peanut sauce is good on everything, so serve the rice, carrots, and tofu with the sauce on the side.

Remember learning to roll-cut vegetables? Eating brown rice every day? Sipping miso soup for breakfast? If this is what you were doing in your commune, then you know how nice it is to return to this food on occasion. It's clean and wholesome and leaves you feeling the same. And even if memory isn't about to take you there, the meal is no less pleasurable. Instead of your thick peanut butter–based sauce, this lighter, greener version includes lots of coriander and mint along with freshly pan-roasted peanuts. It's delicious on many foods, including Skillet-Seared Tofu (page 95) and other Asian-inspired dishes.

I used to drink tea with this dinner, but today I might go for a glass of Austrian Grüner Veltliner, a lively white wine that isn't encumbered with oak.

THE RICE

1 1/2 cups short-grain brown or brown basmati rice

1/2 teaspoon sea salt

THE CARROTS

5 large carrots, peeled

2 teaspoons light or roasted peanut oil

a 1-inch knob of fresh ginger, peeled and sliced into thin strips

soy sauce or tamari to taste

4 scallions, including the greens, thinly cut on the diagonal

sea salt (optional)

THE TOFU

1 carton firm tofu packed in water, drained

sea salt

soy sauce or ponzu sauce

Peanut Sauce (page 200)

1. Rinse the rice, put in a pot with 3 3/4 cups water and the salt, and bring to a boil. Reduce the heat to low and cook, tightly covered, until done, about 40 minutes.

vegetarian suppers

2. Cut the carrots diagonally, rolling a quarter turn each time you slice to make attractive, irregular shaped pieces—thus the roll cut.

3. Heat the oil in a wok or skillet. When hot, add the ginger, then the carrots. Stir-fry for several minutes, then add a few teaspoons soy sauce and stir-fry for 1 minute more. Pour in ½ cup or so of water, cover the pan, and cook until the carrots are tender, 5 or more minutes, depending on their size. Remove the lid, add the scallions, and cook until the liquid is reduced to a glaze. Taste a carrot and season with sea salt if needed.

4. Slice the tofu into ½-inch triangles or rectangles. Heat a large nonstick skillet. Add the tofu, sprinkle it with salt, and cook over medium-high heat until the water cooks out and the tofu starts to color nicely. Turn and cook on the second side until golden, about 10 minutes total. Add a little soy or ponzu sauce to the pan to glaze the tofu.

5. Reheat the carrots if necessary. Serve the rice, the carrots, and the tofu on the same plate and pass the peanut sauce.

Bare-Bones Tofu Curry

SERVES 2 OR 3

Everyone has a standby fast dish, and this is mine. Although minimal, it does accept all kinds of vegetables from green beans to bok choy, tomatoes to winter squash. Steam or stir-fry your chosen vegetable, then add it to the curry at the end.

Serve this curry over rice or rice noodles. For wine, an Alsatian or Oregon Pinot Gris offers lovely fruit with balanced cool-climate acidity.

2 teaspoons roasted or plain peanut oil

1 carton firm tofu packed in water, drained and cubed

sea salt and freshly ground pepper

2 large shallots, sliced

1 can coconut milk, light or regular

1 or 2 teaspoons Thai red curry paste

a few drops soy sauce, preferably mushroom soy

1 tablespoon slivered basil, Thai if possible

1 tablespoon slivered mint leaves, plus 2 or 3 sprigs for garnish

mostly tofu
(and some tempeh)

99

1. Heat a wide nonstick skillet. Film it with a little of the oil and add the tofu. Cook without moving while it gives up its moisture, then, after several minutes, carefully turn it so that it cooks on all sides until pale golden, but still tender. Season with salt and slide it onto a plate.

2. Return the pan to the heat and add the remaining oil. Sauté the shallots until softened and lightly colored, after several minutes. Add the coconut milk to the pan and whisk in the curry paste. Return the tofu to the pan and simmer to heat through. Taste for salt and season with pepper, adding soy for depth, or curry paste for additional heat.

3. Add the basil and mint and any vegetables you are including. Serve spooned over rice, garnished with the sprigs of mint leaves.

Seared Tofu and Mushroom Sauté
with rice noodles

SERVES 4

The filling for mushroom-tofu tortellini from my book *This Can't Be Tofu!* is used to make this silky, dark dish of noodles. The flavors are the same, but the technique has been streamlined (as have the calories) so that you can have a good dinner in less time than it takes to fill a tortellini. The amounts of garlic and tarragon look huge, but they're not. They meld into the dish.

For wine, a spicy, dry Gewürztraminer from Navarro in Mendocino would be a good choice.

You'll be simmering the tofu in water (instead of frying it) so that it will be firm for the sauté. This and the other prep can be done while water is heating for the rice noodles, which take only a few minutes to cook. Sauté the mushrooms, add the sauce, and then toss with the cooked noodles. Be sure you salt things as you go—in spite of the soy sauce, salt is needed!

vegetarian suppers

100

6 ounces wide dried rice noodles

1 carton firm tofu packed in water, drained and diced into small cubes

2 teaspoons mushroom soy sauce or tamari

3 tablespoons naturally brewed soy sauce, such as San-J

2 tablespoons brown sugar

3 tablespoons chopped garlic

1 teaspoon freshly ground black pepper

3 tablespoons chopped tarragon

sea salt

4 teaspoons plain or roasted peanut oil

3/4 to 1 pound assorted fresh mushrooms, including shiitake, if possible

1/2 cup finely diced shallot or onion

4 finely slivered scallions, including the greens

1. Cook the rice noodles in boiling salted water until tender, about 4 minutes. Drain, then rinse with cold water and set aside.

2. Gently simmer the tofu in a skillet of salted water for 2 minutes, then lift the cubes into a colander and set them over a bowl to drain. Mix together the soy sauces and sugar in a small bowl. Chop the garlic, pepper, and tarragon with $\frac{1}{2}$ teaspoon salt.

3. Heat the oil in a wide nonstick skillet. When hot, add the garlic mixture, stir-fry for 20 seconds or so, then add the mushrooms and shallot. Sauté over high heat, stirring often, until their juice has been released and reabsorbed and the mushrooms are brown, about 7 minutes. Add the tofu, followed by the soy-sugar mixture and the cooked noodles. Gently mix everything together and heat through. Taste for salt. Transfer to a platter, garnish with the scallions, and serve.

SERVES 2 TO 3

Tofu and Sugar Snap Peas
in lemon grass broth

If you're cooking rice, start it first. For the tofu, begin by making the broth and prep everything while it simmers. Finish the dish when you're ready to eat.

Aromatic, pretty, and almost indecently fast, this is a very lean dish, too, though you can easily change that by stirring in a spoonful of coconut milk for enrichment. Basically, soft tofu is simmered in enough liquid to float a few somen noodles or moisten some short-grain rice. Some vegetables you might invite to swim with the tofu in its fragrant broth include asparagus tips, fresh pod peas, edamame, baby bok choy, or even diced cherry tomatoes.

For wine, consider a sparkling Asti Spumante. Low in alcohol and a little sweet, with the bubbles it will dance on your palate.

THE BROTH

3 tablespoons chopped fresh or frozen lemon grass

2 slices fresh ginger

grated zest of 1 lime

2 cilantro sprigs plus 2 tablespoons leaves for garnish

sea salt

vegetarian suppers

1 tablespoon soy sauce or fish sauce

1 tablespoon brown sugar or maple syrup

1 carton soft tofu packed in water, drained

1 teaspoon roasted peanut oil

2 garlic cloves, thinly sliced

1/4 red onion, thinly sliced crosswise

2 scallions, including 2 inches of the greens, diagonally sliced

1/2 jalapeño chile, finely diced

a handful of sugar snap peas, edamame, asparagus tips, etc.

1/2 teaspoon ground turmeric

1 cup cooked sticky rice or 1 ounce dry somen noodles, cooked (optional)

lime wedges for serving

1. Put the first 4 broth ingredients in a saucepan with $1\frac{1}{2}$ cups water and a good pinch of salt. Bring to a boil, then simmer, uncovered, for 15 minutes or until reduced to about $\frac{3}{4}$ cup. Strain and add the soy sauce and brown sugar. Taste and adjust the seasonings if needed.

2. While the broth is simmering, drain the tofu, then cut it into cubes.

3. Heat a medium skillet, add the oil, and when it's hot add the garlic, onion, scallions, and chile. Stir-fry over high heat for 30 seconds, then add the peas, turmeric, and tofu. Pour in the broth, then simmer until the peas are bright green and tender-crisp and the tofu is hot, a matter of several minutes. Taste for salt. Add the rice or noodles to the dish, if using, then garnish with the cilantro leaves and serve with the lime wedges.

mostly tofu
(and some tempeh)

Red Sweet Potato Curry
with tofu, bok choy, and caramelized shallots

This dish involves several small, uncomplicated steps. Start with the rice, then go to the sweet potatoes. While they're steaming, cook the tofu, caramelize the shallots, and wilt the greens. Then bring everything together over a bowl of rice.

My neighborhood market seems to have a lead on extra-small sweet potatoes whose size is ideal for this dish. But if large tubers are what you have—and no doubt they will be—cut them into long wedges or other shapes pleasing to you. Syrupy mushroom soy sauce vastly broadens the flavor of the dish, turning the sauce a caramel-candy shade of brown.

For wine, try a weighty Pinot Gris from Alsace with crisp acidity that can dance with the richness, sweetness, and spice in this dish.

Sweet Potato Curry with Tempeh

In place of the tofu, steam one or two blocks of tempeh for 15 minutes, then cut them into thin rectangles and brown them in roasted peanut oil on both sides before adding them to the sauce.

brown or white Basmati Rice (page 206)

1 generous pound small sweet potatoes, scrubbed

1 can coconut milk

1 to 2 teaspoons Thai red curry paste or more to taste

½ cup chopped cilantro, plus sprigs for garnish

1 carton firm tofu packed in water, drained and cut into 1-inch cubes

1 tablespoon roasted peanut oil, plus a little for the tofu

sea salt

a few teaspoons mushroom soy sauce or San-J soy sauce

6 large shallots, peeled and sliced into rounds

4 baby bok choy, cut lengthwise into sixths

1 lime, quartered

1. Start your rice. Cut the sweet potatoes lengthwise into wedges about ¾ inch wide. Steam them over boiling water until tender, about 20 minutes.

2. Heat the coconut milk with 1 cup water in a wide skillet. Stir in the curry paste and chopped cilantro. Add the cooked sweet potatoes and lower the heat.

3. Meanwhile, put the tofu in a single layer in a nonstick skillet over medium heat. Cook until the water has evaporated and the tofu is golden, about 5 minutes, adding a little oil for flavor and to give it a crisp surface. Season with salt, douse with a few teaspoons mushroom soy sauce, and shuffle the pan until the tofu cubes are coated evenly and a dark lustrous brown. After 3 to 5 minutes add the tofu to the sweet potatoes, wipe out the pan, and return it to the heat.

4. Add 2 teaspoons of the remaining peanut oil to the pan. When hot, add the shallots. Season with salt and cook over medium-high heat for several minutes, stirring occasionally, until golden, 3 to 4 minutes. Set aside. Simmer the bok choy in salted water until tender, 4 to 5 minutes, then remove and toss with the remaining 1 teaspoon peanut oil.

5. Serve the sweet potatoes and their sauce over rice, garnished with the bok choy, shallots, cilantro sprigs, and lime wedges.

Spicy Tofu
with thai basil and coconut rice cakes

SERVES 2 TO 3

Thai basil, with its warm, spicy overtones and beautiful purple-edged leaves, is the one to use here, but any other variety will work too. Use whatever variety you have and keep this dish in mind for when you do find Thai basil at your market.

An off-dry Riesling, such as a German Kabinett, would be good with this dairy-free dish.

Coconut Rice Cakes (recipe follows)

1 teaspoon brown sugar or palm sugar

2 tablespoons light soy sauce, such as Kikkoman, or more as needed

4 teaspoons roasted peanut oil

1 carton firm tofu packed in water, drained and cut into large cubes

sea salt and freshly ground pepper

2 limes, 1 halved and 1 quartered

2 plump garlic cloves, chopped

3 large shallots, thinly sliced crosswise

1 jalapeño chile, veins and seeds removed first if you want to minimize the heat, diced

1/2 can (1 scant cup) coconut milk

1/2 teaspoon ground turmeric

a handful of Thai basil leaves, torn into large pieces if large, plus sprigs for garnish

12 mint leaves, torn into pieces

1 red jalapeño chile, sliced diagonally, or 2 Thai peppers for more heat

Cook the rice at least several hours ahead of time so that it can firm up. If that isn't possible, just make the rice and serve it hot from the pot, molded, if you like, in a cup or some pretty-shaped dish. The leftover coconut milk from the rice is used with the tofu. If you're making rice cakes, start heating them when you begin cooking the tofu so that they'll be ready at the same time.

mostly tofu
(and some tempeh)

1. Make the rice cakes. When cooled, cut them into triangles and start frying them slowly in a little light peanut oil. Stir the sugar into the soy sauce and set aside.

2. Heat a teaspoon of the roasted peanut oil in a medium nonstick skillet and add the tofu. It will sizzle as the water cooks off but will then begin to color. After several minutes, turn the pieces so that they color on all sides. When golden, after about 4 minutes, season with a few pinches of salt, some pepper, and the juice of ½ lime. Slide the tofu onto a plate and return the pan to the heat.

3. Add the rest of the oil to the pan. Add the garlic, shallots, and chile and stir-fry for 30 seconds. Pour in the soy sauce mixture, then add the coconut milk and turmeric. Squeeze the second half of the lime over all and return the tofu to the pan. When the sauce and tofu are hot, turn off the heat. Taste for salt and add more salt or soy sauce as needed. Season with pepper and stir in the basil and mint leaves.

4. Arrange the rice cakes on plates with the seed-coated side facing up. Or, if you just cooked the rice, pack it into a ramekin or a mold, then turn it out, one on each plate. Add the tofu and its sauce and serve, garnished with a sprig of the Thai basil leaves, the jalapeño, and the lime quarters.

Coconut Rice Cakes

1½ cups basmati rice

½ can (1 scant cup) coconut milk

2 pinches of saffron threads

½ teaspoon ground turmeric

sea salt and freshly ground pepper

4 slender scallions, including the greens, thinly sliced

⅓ cup sesame seeds (black and white are nice)

light peanut or sesame oil for frying

1. Rinse the rice. Bring 2 cups water and the coconut milk to a boil with the saffron and turmeric. Add the rice and ¾ teaspoon salt, cover the pan, and cook over low heat until the rice is done, about 20 minutes.

2. Using a fork, gently toss in the scallions, season with pepper, then turn the rice into a 9- by 12-inch pan. Scatter the sesame seeds over the rice, then place plastic wrap over it and press firmly. Refrigerate until well chilled, then cut into diamonds or other shapes.

Stir-Fried Sesame Broccoli
and tofu with glass noodles

First press the tofu and soak the mushrooms and the noodles. While they're soaking, chop and dice the vegetables. Cook the tofu, then start your stir-fry. Note that the soy sauce and both the oils are used at various stages in this dish.

This is about as much as you can fit into a huge skillet, but four will eat it all. The secret to making this easy is the same as for any stir-fry: get all the bits and pieces—the marinade, the sesame seeds, the seasonings—gathered together before you start to cook.

A dry Pinot Blanc would be a good partner for this homey dish.

1 carton firm tofu packed in water, drained

2 fistfuls of bean thread noodles (about 5 ounces)

1 pound or more broccoli

sea salt

6 tablespoons soy sauce

4 teaspoons roasted sesame oil

8 dried shiitake mushrooms, covered with near-boiling water

5 teaspoons light sesame or peanut oil

1½-inch knob of fresh ginger, peeled and minced

1 large garlic clove, minced

4 scallions, including the greens, sliced diagonally

2 tablespoons mirin or 1½ tablespoons light brown sugar

¼ cup toasted sesame seeds

1. Set the tofu in a colander, put a heavy object, such as a can of beans, on top, and set aside. Heat a pot of water for the broccoli. When hot, scoop some out and pour it over the noodles in a bowl. Let them stand until softened, about 10 minutes, then drain.

2. Cut the broccoli into florets. Thickly peel the bulk of the stems and then cut them into thin coins. When the water comes to a boil, add salt and the broccoli and cook for 1 minute. Drain and rinse under cold water.

3. Remove the tofu from under its weight, slice it into ¾-inch cubes, and put them in a glass pie plate. Mix 2 tablespoons of the soy sauce with 2 teaspoons of the roasted sesame oil and pour it over the tofu. Remove and discard the stems from the mushrooms, slice the caps, strain and reserve the soaking water.

4. When you're ready to eat, heat a wok or wide nonstick skillet over medium-high heat, and add 2 teaspoons of the light sesame oil. When hot, add the tofu. Cook, without stirring, until it begins to color, after a few minutes. Then give the pieces a nudge and turn them so that they brown all sides. Add any remaining marinade to the pan to glaze the tofu, season it with salt, then set the tofu aside on a plate. Rinse out the skillet.

5. Heat the rest of the light sesame oil in the skillet. Add the ginger, garlic, and scallions and stir-fry for 30 seconds, then add the mushrooms, along with their soaking water. Cook for 2 to 3 minutes, then add the broccoli, noodles, and tofu. Combine the remaining soy sauce with the mirin and pour it over the vegetables. When heated through, toss with the toasted seeds, drizzle with the rest of the dark sesame oil, and serve.

Sweet-and-Sour Tofu (or Tempeh)
with summer vegetables and black rice

SERVES 3 TO 4

Red and golden vegetables against a backdrop of black rice ensures plenty of visual drama. Roma tomatoes, cherry, Sun Golds, orange, yellow, or green types—they're all good, and they make this speedy little dish extra pretty. But looks aren't everything; this stir-fry tastes good, too, whether you use tofu or tempeh. If using tempeh, steam the whole piece for 15 minutes, then cut it into bite-sized pieces and brown in peanut oil before adding them to the sauce. Tempeh will drink up the sauce, so add it toward the end.

Serve a palate-cleansing Riesling, Old or New World, with this summer dish—a Bonny Doon Pacific Rim Riesling from California or a Trimbach Riesling from Alsace.

First start the rice since it takes a good 35 minutes. Prepare the various parts of the dish, then, when the rice is ready, finish cooking it.

Black Rice (page 207)

2 tablespoons balsamic or Chinese black vinegar

3 tablespoons tamari or naturally brewed soy sauce, such as San-J

2 scant tablespoons light brown, maple, or palm sugar

sea salt

1 cup fresh tomatoes, chopped neatly in large pieces

1 or 2 handfuls of skinny green beans, tipped and tailed

1 carton firm tofu packed in water, drained and cut into cubes

4 teaspoons roasted peanut oil

1 jalapeño chile, minced

1 tablespoon chopped fresh ginger

1 large sweet onion, cut into 1-inch dice

1 yellow bell pepper, cut into inch-wide slices or squares

2 teaspoons chopped garlic

1 teaspoon cornstarch mixed with ¾ cup Stock for Stir-Fries (page 210) or water

mostly tofu
(and some tempeh)

1. Start the rice. Mix the vinegar, tamari, sugar, and ½ teaspoon salt in a medium bowl. Add the tomatoes and set them aside.

2. Bring a large skillet of water to a boil. Add salt and the beans and cook just until tender-firm. Lift them out, then rinse to stop the cooking. Lower the heat, then add the tofu and simmer until firm, about 2 minutes. Remove to a plate. Empty the skillet and return it to the stove.

3. Turn the heat on high and add the oil. When it's hot, add the chile and ginger. Stir-fry for 30 seconds, then add the onion and pepper and stir-fry until translucent and seared on the edges, about 2 minutes. Add the garlic, tomatoes, beans, sauce, and then the tofu. Give the cornstarch and stock a stir, add it to the pan, and simmer until bubbling and hot. Serve with the black rice.

Star Anise–Glazed Tempeh
with stir-fried peppers

This easy, colorful stir-fry is one of the tastiest ways I've found to cook tempeh. I serve it with rice—black, white, or brown—garnished with plump toasted cashews and accompanied by a dry sparkling California rosé from Handley cellars in Mendocino or from Domaine Chandon in Napa.

Start your rice first so that it's ready when everything else is done.

Black Rice (page 207) or Basmati Rice (page 206)

THE MARINADE AND TEMPEH

¼ cup naturally brewed soy sauce, such as San-J

¼ cup mirin

2 tablespoons brown or white sugar

1 tablespoon maple syrup

¼ teaspoon five-spice powder or 1 3-inch cinnamon stick plus 2 star anise

1 package of tempeh, each piece cut into four squares

4 teaspoons roasted peanut oil

1 garlic clove, chopped

1 tablespoon minced ginger

1 bunch of scallions, including several inches of the greens, slivered diagonally

4 heaping cups finely sliced red cabbage

1 red bell pepper, very thinly sliced

1 yellow bell pepper, very thinly sliced

sea salt

a handful of chopped cilantro

⅓ cup roasted whole cashews or roasted peanuts

1. Start the rice.

2. Bring the ingredients for the marinade (minus the tempeh) to a boil in a medium skillet with 1 cup water. Cook at a lively pace for 4 minutes, then turn off the heat. Cut each of the 4 tempeh squares into triangles, then put them in the hot marinade for 4 minutes, turning once. Remove and set aside, reserving the marinade.

3. Heat 2 teaspoons of the oil in a wide nonstick skillet or a wok. When hot, brown the marinated tempeh, about a minute on each side. Add a few tablespoons of the re-

mostly tofu (and some tempeh)

111

served marinade and allow it to bubble up and glaze the tempeh. Set aside on a plate, rinse out the skillet, then return it to the stove.

4. Heat the rest of the oil. When it's hot, add the garlic, ginger, and scallions, stir-fry for a few seconds, then add the cabbage and peppers. Season with a little salt and stir-fry until just wilted, after several minutes. Add the remaining marinade and the cilantro and simmer for 30 seconds.

5. Mound the cooked rice on 4 plates. Rest the tempeh pieces on the rice, tuck the stir-fry between them, and drizzle the remaining sauce over all. Add the cashews last, then serve.

Vegan Migas

These are seasoned just like the migas made with eggs on page 119, but with extra fresh chile, chipotle, and cilantro to overcome the neutrality of the tofu. As with the others, you can serve them with a side of black beans or pinto beans (page 208). I'd have something silky and sweet for dessert, such as a sliced mango with lime, and instead of wine, quaff sweetened jamaica flower tea.

1 carton soft tofu packed in water	4 scallions, including the greens, chopped
3 stale corn tortillas, torn into strips	sea salt
1 tablespoon oil	¼ cup chopped cilantro
pinch of ground turmeric	2 Roma tomatoes, diced
1 or 2 jalapeño or serrano chiles, finely diced, seeded if less heat is desired	½ cup grated nondairy cheese
½ teaspoon ground chipotle chile or smoky Spanish paprika or more to taste	Salsa Ranchera (page 118) and warm tortillas for serving

1. Drain the tofu while you gather the rest of your ingredients. Crisp the tortilla strips in a little oil in a nonstick skillet or toast until crisp.

2. Heat a medium nonstick skillet and add the tablespoon of oil. When hot, crumble the tofu into the pan into pieces about the size of the curds of scrambled eggs. Sprinkle with turmeric, add the chiles, chipotle powder, and scallions, and season with ½ teaspoon salt. Cook over medium heat, stirring, until the water remaining in the tofu has cooked away, but not so long that the tofu turns hard, 4 to 6 minutes. It should remain tender, like eggs.

3. Add the cilantro and tomatoes, followed by the cheese and tortilla chips. Continue cooking until the cheese has melted. Serve with a slotted spoon so that any water from the tofu remains in the pan. Serve with salsa and warm tortillas.

eggs for supper

*N*othing is faster to cook than an egg, not even the piece of toast you're going to enjoy with it. And supper is a perfect time for eggs. Naturally, none of these recipes is vegan.

Eggs give busy people a way to eat real food quickly and easily, and even soufflés take little time to prepare. In fact, such dishes are valuable additions to anyone's supper repertoire. Soufflés are dramatic, frittatas sturdy (and good hot or cold), and baked eggs offer comfort and ease mixed with the feeling that you're doing something special for yourself. But a fried egg sandwich or scrambled eggs will always be there for you when anything else requires more than you've got to give.

Given that there are entire books, and very large ones at that, devoted to the possibilities of the egg, it's hardly an easy task to choose just a dozen or so recipes. But here they are, a group that includes a few old favorites, like the reliably great onion frittata with its glaze of sherry vinegar, but mostly new recipes, such as eggs baked over smoky potatoes or a flat corn omelet. And while eggs baked over mushrooms may seem old-fashioned, they shouldn't, because they're ridiculously easy to prepare and make a nice change from fried or scrambled eggs.

6

A Fried Egg Sandwich

A fried egg sandwich fills the void at any time of day quickly and pleasantly. They're seldom seen anymore, though on a recent trip to the Florida Keys, I was surprised to find fried egg sandwiches on many café menus, usually adorned with cheese, bacon, ham, or tomatoes, smashed between pieces of insipid toast. While the extras can be great, it's the combination of crunchy toast and a slightly runny egg that is completely satisfying.

If you're in the mood, why not drink a sparkling wine? With bubbles and acidity that wrap around food and enliven your mouth, sparkling wines can be for every day, not just for special occasions.

2 slices good-quality bread, such as whole wheat, sourdough, sturdy white, or semolina

2 teaspoons butter

2 eggs

sea salt and freshly ground pepper

Toast the bread. Melt 2 teaspoons butter in a small nonstick skillet. When it sizzles, crack your eggs into the pan, salt and pepper the top, and cook for a minute or so. Then turn the eggs and cook them on the second side until the yolks are as runny or firm as you like them. Slide them onto the toast, top with the second slice, cut in half, and serve.

And now for those extras

- Lay thin slices of your favorite cheese over the hot toast. A sharp Cheddar is always good, but you might try something more adventurous, such as an aged goat, a Tuscan pecorino, or a slice of manchego.
- Add a sliced ripe tomato.
- Spread some pureed chipotle chile in adobo or some harissa over the toast if you go for heat and spice.
- For robust flavors other than chile, spread your toast with tapenade, Romesco Sauce (page 198), Chimichurri Sauce (page 198), or Marjoram Pesto (page 175).

Scrambled Eggs in a Tortilla
with two salsas

What makes scrambled eggs and a tortilla more than just something easy to throw together is having a good salsa, and there are some pretty good commercial ones on the market. Or take a few minutes to make your own instead of reaching for a jar. I offer a choice of salsas here, a fresh one made with ripe tomatoes and an avocado and a cooked one, a salsa ranchera, which is, of course, classic with huevos rancheros. The tart Tomatilla Salsa on page 201 is also excellent with eggs.

I like beer with chile and salsa, but a Kabinett Riesling from Germany, with its low alcohol, zippy acidity, and lively fruit, would also be good with the eggs and avocado.

It takes a bit of coordination to have the tortillas and eggs arrive properly cooked at the same moment. To help things along, have your table set, make your salsa(s) first, then cook the eggs and warm the tortillas at the same time. Even better, have someone else take care of the tortillas while you make the eggs.

Salsa Cruda with Avocado (page 118)

Salsa Ranchera (page 118)

6 to 8 eggs

sea salt

3 tablespoons butter or olive oil

crumbled feta cheese, fresh goat cheese, or grated Jack cheese

chopped cilantro

4 large whole wheat tortillas

1. Make the salsas. If you have refrigerated them, give them time to warm up to room temperature before serving them with the warm eggs.

2. Heat a griddle or large skillet and have a clean dish towel at hand. Beat the eggs in a bowl with ½ teaspoon salt and 2 tablespoons water. Melt the butter in a wide skillet. When foamy, pour in the eggs, lower the heat, and cook, stirring constantly until the curds form and are as wet or as dry as you like them. Add the cheese and the cilantro toward the end. At the same time, start warming the tortillas by placing them on the hot griddle or skillet, turning them to warm both sides. As they get hot, stack and wrap them in the towel.

3. Divide the eggs among the warm tortillas, spoon over the salsa, fold the tortillas around the eggs, and serve. If using the warm salsa ranchera, fold the tortilla over the eggs, then smother it with the salsa and add a little extra cheese.

Salsa Cruda with Avocado

5 plum tomatoes or 3 ripe medium tomatoes

¼ cup finely diced red or white onion

1 jalapeño chile, finely diced, seeded first if
     you want less heat

12 cilantro sprigs, chopped

1 avocado, finely diced

pureed or ground chipotle chile to taste
     (optional)

juice of 1 lime or a splash of beer

sea salt

Halve the tomatoes lengthwise, squeeze the seeds into a strainer, then chop the flesh into small pieces. Put the tomato into a bowl with the onion, chile, cilantro, and avocado. Add lime juice or a splash of beer and season with salt to taste.

Salsa Ranchera

6 large ripe tomatoes

2 plump garlic cloves, unpeeled

2 to 4 jalapeño or serrano chiles (the latter
     being hotter)

2 tablespoons sunflower seed oil

sea salt

Put the tomatoes, garlic, and chiles in a cast-iron skillet over medium heat. Cook, turning everything, until the skins are blistered and charred in places. Remove the chiles and garlic as they cook. Expect the tomatoes to get a little mushy. Put the tomatoes with their scorched skins, the garlic (now peeled), and the chiles, (stems removed), in a blender and puree until smooth. Heat the oil in the skillet, pour in the puree, season with ½ teaspoon salt, and cook over medium-high heat, stirring and scraping the pan, until the sauce has thickened somewhat, about 10 minutes. Taste for salt.

Migas

Scrambled eggs studded with crisp corn tortilla shards are a Tex-Mex breakfast favorite that's great at any time of day, not just in the morning. They're hearty, tasty, and practical, which is why I've included them, along with a vegan version on page 113.

Transform this breakfast into supper by starting with a bowl of posole or by including a side of pinto beans or black beans, along with bowls of Salsa Ranchera (page 118) or the sharper Tomatillo Salsa (page 201). To drink? Beer, Riesling, or iced tea.

3 stale corn tortillas, torn or cut into strips

1 tablespoon oil or butter for the eggs

3 scallions, including the greens, chopped

1 jalapeño or serrano chile, finely diced, seeded if less heat is desired

several pinches of ground chipotle chile or smoky Spanish paprika

4 eggs, beaten with 2 teaspoons water

2 Roma tomatoes, diced

$\frac{1}{2}$ cup grated Monterey Jack or Cheddar cheese

several tablespoons chopped cilantro

sea salt

Salsa Ranchera (page 118) or Tomatillo Salsa (page 201)

warm tortillas and black beans (page 208) for serving

1. First crisp the tortilla strips or fry them in a little oil until crisp.

2. Heat the oil in a nonstick skillet over medium heat. Add the scallions, fresh chile, and dried chipotle, and cook over medium heat until the scallions are limp. Then pour in the beaten eggs, lower the heat, and stir until soft curds form. Just before the eggs are finished, stir in the tortilla pieces, tomatoes, cheese, and cilantro. Season with salt and serve with a salsa, warm tortillas, and black beans.

eggs for supper

Eggs
baked on a bed of sautéed mushrooms and croutons

While the oven is heating, brown the bread cubes and sauté the mushrooms. By then the oven will be ready. Don't use a convection setting—the moving air will blow on the yolks and cook them unevenly.

When you're tired but want to cook a little and not just heat something up, this offers just the right amount of involvement to feel as if you've done something nice for yourself. I like the texture the bread provides, but you can bake eggs over all kinds of things, such as stewed summer tomatoes, sautéed peppers, leftover ratatouille, braised spinach, and so forth.

With a glass of wine and a salad with a good mustardy dressing, this is my idea of a perfect supper for one or two people (not that it can't be multiplied). And it justifies having a number of single-serving, low-sided terra-cotta gratin dishes. These eggs call for a simple workingman's Burgundy from Côte Chalonnaise, such as Aubert Villaine's Mercurey, or a Pinot Noir from Santa Maria Valley in Santa Barbara County, such as Au Bon Climat.

2 tablespoons butter

2 slices bread, cut into small cubes

1 tablespoon olive oil

$^1\!/_3$ cup finely diced shallot or onion

6 large brown mushrooms, cremini or portobello, thickly sliced (about $^1\!/_2$ pound)

1 tablespoon chopped parsley

2 teaspoons chopped marjoram or rosemary

sea salt and freshly ground pepper

2 generous teaspoons tomato paste

$^3\!/_4$ cup red wine, preferably the wine you'll be drinking

2 or 4 eggs

1. Preheat the oven to 400°F. Lightly butter 2 shallow baking dishes and set them on a sheet pan.

2. Melt half the butter in a medium skillet, add the cubed bread, and toss it about the pan. Cook over low heat, stirring frequently, until it's golden and crisp, about 8 to 10 minutes, but not hard. Divide the croutons between the dishes.

3. Heat the oil and remaining butter in a wide skillet over medium heat. Add the shallot and cook, stirring frequently, for about 3 minutes. Raise the heat, then add the mushrooms, most of the herbs, and a few pinches of salt. Sauté until the mushrooms have started to brown, about 5 minutes. Stir in the tomato paste, then add the wine and immediately scrape the pan to release the juicy bits. Lower the heat and simmer until a

few tablespoons of juice remain. Season with salt and pepper and divide the mushrooms between the dishes.

4. Break one or two eggs over the croutons and mushrooms and add a pinch of salt and some pepper. Bake until the whites are set, about 15 minutes, and the yolks are as firm as you like. Remove, sprinkle the rest of the herbs over the top, and serve.

Eggs
over smoky potatoes

Start the potatoes, then finish the dish by cracking the eggs over them and finishing them in the oven or on top of the stove.

That smoky Spanish pimentón does wonders for foods that might otherwise be cooked with sausage, such as these eggs and potatoes, inspired by a recipe in Marie Simmons's book *The Good Egg*. While you can finish the eggs on the stove, I think it makes an especially handsome presentation if you transfer the potatoes to a shallow-sided earthernware gratin dish, bake the eggs in the oven, and bring the whole, gorgeous dish to the table. This recipe is as easy to make for one as it is for a crowd.

A bit intense for an early-morning breakfast perhaps, these lusty eggs are great for supper at any time of year. In summer I'd serve them with sautéed peppers and in winter with a lively salad of cauliflower, green olives, and green peppers, ending with a cooling orange compote for dessert. For wine, stay with the Spanish influence and choose a Ribera del Duero for a red, or an Albariño for a white.

approximately 2 pounds potatoes, any
    variety, peeled and cut into ½-inch dice
2 tablespoons olive oil
sea salt
½ to 1 teaspoon Spanish smoked paprika
    (pimentón), to taste

1 garlic clove, minced
4 scallions, including a few inches of the
    greens, thinly sliced
4 or more eggs
minced parsley to finish

1. If you're using russet or baking potatoes, put them in cold water as you work to draw out some of the starch. Drain them and blot them dry before cooking.

2. Heat the oil in a large, well-seasoned cast-iron or nonstick skillet. Add the potatoes to the pan and cook over medium heat, turning them every so often so they brown on all sides. When they're tender, after 15 minutes or so, season them with salt, toss them with the smoked paprika, garlic, and scallions, and cook for 1 minute more.

3. Break the eggs over the potatoes. You can add more as long as there is room for them. Cover the pan and cook over medium-low heat until the whites are set, about 5 minutes, or longer, if you want the yolks set as well. Sprinkle with the parsley and serve.

Or preheat the oven to 375°F and transfer the potatoes to a lightly oiled terra-cotta gratin dish. Break the eggs over them, then bake until set and as done as you like, 15 to 20 minutes. Garnish with the parsley and serve in their dish.

Ricotta Omelet
with crisp bread crumbs and marjoram

Sauté the bread crumbs first so that you can include some in the beaten eggs. Preheat the broiler, and you're ready.

By itself, a ricotta omelet can be very soothing, but it can also take on a range of accompaniments from fiery salsas to sautéed tomatoes, roasted asparagus to feisty greens. I use a good whole-milk ricotta, such as that made by Calabro, Redwood Hill Farm, and other small dairies. Whole-milk ricotta has the best texture and flavor, but go with the lower-fat version if that's what you like.

For wine, consider an herbaceous Sauvignon Blanc from New Zealand or a light fruity red such as Beaujolais. For a more serious red, a Gigondas (Grenache-based) from the southern Rhône would be in order.

vegetarian suppers

1 large piece chewy rustic bread, crusts
    removed

4 or 5 large eggs

sea salt and freshly ground pepper

1 cup ricotta cheese

$1/4$ cup grated Parmigiano-Reggiano, plus
    extra for the top

1 tablespoon chopped fresh marjoram

1 small garlic clove, crushed and minced
    with a few pinches of salt

2 tablespoons butter

1. Preheat the broiler. Tear the bread by hand or pulse it in a food processor to make irregularly sized bread crumbs. Toast them in a dry skillet or in melted butter until golden and crisp.

2. Beat the eggs with a scant $1/2$ teaspoon salt and a little pepper, then stir in the ricotta, Parmesan, most of the marjoram, the garlic, and half the bread crumbs. There's no need to make the mixture utterly smooth.

3. Heat the butter until foamy in an 8- or 10-inch skillet, add the egg mixture and give it a stir, then lower the heat and cook until just a bit wet on top, about 6 minutes. Lightly brown the top under the broiler, then slide the frittata onto a plate. Sprinkle with the bread crumbs and garnish with an extra grating of Parmesan, the rest of the marjoram, and a little pepper.

Variation with sage

Toward the end of the summer, marjoram, my favorite herb, starts tasting oddly like nutmeg and way too sweet. That's when it's time to switch to a more autumnal herb, sage. Roughly chop a dozen sage leaves. Heat a tablespoon of olive oil or melt butter in a small skillet, then add the sage and a few grinds of freshly cracked pepper, and cook just to warm the sage. Add the bread crumbs and crisp them, then continue with the recipe as given.

Corn Omelet
with smoked mozzarella and basil

Easy to multiply, utterly simple, and delicious, this flat omelet is especially good when made with smoky mozzarella and fresh corn. And if you aren't up to inverting the eggs, and all of that, this combination of elements makes terrific scrambled eggs, too. Grilled corn as well as fresh is excellent here, so keep that in mind if you happen to be grilling. Frozen, however convenient, simply lacks the magic that fresh has when it's being featured in such a forward, simple dish.

Just-sliced tomatoes with crunchy Malden sea salt, olive oil, a few drops of vinegar, and toast make a simple and pleasing summer supper. With the corn and cheese, a New World Chardonnay such as Sanford from Santa Barbara would be a good choice.

Should you use fresh rather than smoked mozzarella, dice it, then let it rest on paper towels to release its water; otherwise your eggs will be watery.

1 ear of corn, grilled or raw, the kernels sliced off the cob

2 eggs, beaten with 1 tablespoon water

sea salt and freshly ground pepper

several basil leaves, slivered

about 1 ounce grated smoked mozzarella cheese

1 tablespoon butter

1. If you're using new corn, put it in a small skillet with a few tablespoons water and simmer until tender and heated through, a few minutes. Drain, then add it to the beaten eggs and season with a couple pinches of salt, some pepper, and the basil. Stir in the cheese.

2. Wipe out the pan and melt the butter. When it foams, pour in the eggs and give them a couple of quick stirs around the pan. Cover with the plate you plan to eat from (it will warm it), lower the heat, and cook the eggs until pale gold on the bottom. Slide the omelet onto the plate, invert the pan over it, grasp the whole unit, and flip it over. Slide the omelet back into the pan and cook the second side just until it sets, about a minute. Tip it onto your plate, add a sliced tomato salad, and serve.

Spinach Frittata

I consider one of life's luxuries to be a huge bag of glistening spinach leaves from the farmers' market to dip into at will. In winter, I turn to organic baby spinach leaves that are packed so that the leaves are fresh but dry, ideal in this recipe. How many this frittata feeds depends on appetites and side dishes. While I find a quarter is sufficient, my husband will eat a half.

Sautéed mushrooms are a quick and natural pairing with these eggs, as are carrots cooked with fresh thyme or dill.

You can eat it at room temperature—take it on a picnic or to the porch, along with a tomato salad and a crusty baguette. If serving the frittata on the cool side, drink it with an herbaceous Sauvignon Blanc from New Zealand. If warm from the pan, go for a more fruit-forward Sauvignon Blanc from Sonoma's Russian River.

8 to 10 ounces stemmed baby spinach leaves

2 tablespoons butter

sea salt and freshly ground pepper

4 eggs

2 scallions, including 3 inches of the greens, finely sliced

3 ounces crumbled firm goat cheese, such as Boucheron or Redwood Hill Farm's Bucheret

1. Put the spinach in a large skillet with a teaspoon or so of the butter, season with a few pinches of salt, and add a tablespoon of water to create a little steam. Cook over medium heat until wilted and tender, about 3 minutes. Drain, then chop coarsely.

2. Whisk the eggs in a medium bowl with several pinches of salt and some pepper. Stir in the scallions, cheese, and spinach.

3. Melt the remaining butter in a 10-inch nonstick skillet. When it foams, swirl it around the pan, coating the sides. Add the eggs, reduce the heat to low, then cover the pan and cook until golden and puffed, about 8 minutes. If, at this time, it's cooked to your taste, slide it out onto a serving plate without turning it over. If you like your eggs cooked more firmly, slide the frittata onto a plate, invert the skillet over it, then, grasping both the plate and the skillet in your hands, invert the whole thing. Cook the second side for a few more minutes, then slide the frittata onto the plate, cut into quarters, and serve.

- While spinach is at the heart of this frittata, it needn't necessarily be there by itself. Arugula, sorrel, amaranth, and other greens, a few leaves or a handful, add mystery to an otherwise straightforward dish when you cook them with the spinach.

- Instead of the pungent goat cheese with spinach, make this frittata with a sheep's or goat's milk feta and season the eggs with a few tablespoons finely chopped dill and 1 minced lovage leaf, if available.

- If you love cilantro, you might also include a handful, finely chopped, as well as or instead of the dill.

Onion Frittata
glazed with sherry vinegar

While the onions are cooking, you can easily get the rest of your meal together.

This frittata from *The Savory Way* is one I've taught many times to enthusiastic eaters, who always respond to the perfume of the sizzling sherry vinegar and butter at the end. This vinegar-butter combination does wonders for a plate of fried eggs as well. I do like this high and dense, but if you make three or four smaller, thinner frittatas, you can use them as the filling for a delicious sandwich.

I've taken the walnuts out of the original version and suggest that you instead toss them into an arugula salad topped with thinly shaved Gruyère cheese. A southern Rhône blend of Grenache and Syrah as found in Côtes-du-Rhône, or an Oregon Pinot Noir, such as St. Innocent, would suit this dish well.

1½ tablespoons olive oil	⅛ teaspoon ground cloves
2 pounds onions (3 large), peeled, quartered, then sliced crosswise about ¼ inch thick	6 eggs, whisked with 2 tablespoons water
2 tablespoons sherry vinegar	2 tablespoons chopped parsley, plus extra for garnish
sea salt and freshly ground pepper	3 tablespoons butter

1. Warm the olive oil in a 10-inch skillet, add the onions, and cook over medium heat, stirring occasionally, until golden, about 30 minutes. Add half the vinegar, raise the heat, and reduce while stirring. Season with ¾ teaspoon salt, a few twists of pepper, and the ground cloves. Preheat the broiler.

2. Add several pinches of salt to the eggs and beat with the water. Then stir in the onions and parsley. Melt half the butter in a 10-inch skillet. When it's sizzling, add the eggs. Cover and cook over low heat until the eggs are set, 8 to 10 minutes. Slide the pan under the broiler until the eggs are set and golden. Tip the frittata onto a serving dish and return the pan to the stove.

3. Add the remaining butter and, when it begins to foam, add the remaining vinegar. Slide the pan back and forth to emulsify the two, then pour it over the eggs. Add a few pinches of chopped parsley and serve.

Souffléed Omelet

"This is like eating a cloud" writes Ann Clark, speaking of her wonderful boozy dessert soufflé in *Quick Cuisine,* one of my favorite cookbooks. Savory versions are also cloud-like and unbelievably easy to make in return for so much drama. This soufflé-omelet is a great standby for when you need an instant dinner that has some panache—eggs are almost always on hand, and it takes less than 15 minutes.

Enjoy this puffy wonder plain or with a little dusting of freshly grated Parmesan cheese. Or fold it over vegetables, such as simmered or roasted asparagus, leftover ratatouille, sautéed greens, artichokes, or sautéed peppers. Have a green salad afterward, when the drama is over. The wine will depend on any fillings you add, but if you're eating this by itself, you might go with an unoaked white with citrus notes, such as an Arneis, from Piedmont.

Unless you're serving the omelet plain, make the vegetable fillings first, since the eggs take only about 12 minutes after the oven is heated.

4 eggs, separated

sea salt and freshly ground pepper

1 tablespoon butter or olive oil

a chunk of Parmesan cheese for grating

(optional)

1. Preheat the oven to 350°F. Whisk the egg yolks with 2 tablespoons water, ½ teaspoon salt, and a little pepper. Whisk the egg whites until they form firm but moist peaks. Don't let them get dry and hard or the omelet will not be its best.

2. Melt the butter or heat the oil in a 10-inch nonstick or cast-iron skillet. When it foams, remove the pan from the heat, fold the whites into the yolks, then slide the whole mound into the skillet. Cook over low heat just until the bottom is set, for 1 minute, then slide the pan into the oven and bake until puffed, golden, and set, 10 to 12 minutes.

3. If serving plain, grate a little cheese over the top if desired and slide the omelet onto a plate. If adding a cooked vegetable, spoon it over half the omelet, a little to one side of center, then fold the other half over it, slide the whole thing onto an oval plate, and serve.

eggs for supper

Once- and Twice-Baked Goat Cheese Soufflés

Soufflés never fail to make a dramatic entrance and one of the most satisfying suppers there is. In fact, I think that everyone should know how to make a soufflé, not only because it's just so lovely to behold and you'll get lots of credit as its creator but also because a soufflé is terribly easy and fast to make. They are far more sturdy and flexible than you might imagine—at least until you take them out of the oven. Then you need to move them to waiting warm plates without delay. However, if you're using the twice-baked method, you can finish them when you need them—ideal for when you want to put individual soufflés on a plate with something else, such as the Beet and Tomato Ragout on page 33.

Once-Baked, Regular Soufflé

A cheese soufflé, especially one made with a sharp goat cheese, is one of my favorite suppers. This amount will serve four, but I'm afraid I've found that two of us can polish it off without difficulty. Lentils cooked in red wine, buttered, and peppered make a fine accompaniment along with a salad. Sauvignon Blanc from France's Loire Valley is a classic pairing with goat cheese. But with the presence of the heartier lentils, you could go with light-bodied, pleasing reds, such as one from the Loire Valley or a Cabernet Franc from the village of Chinon or Bourgueil.

$1\frac{1}{2}$ cups milk

aromatics: 2 onion slices, 1 thyme sprig,
    1 bay leaf, and 1 garlic clove, crushed

sea salt and freshly ground white pepper

3 tablespoons butter

3 tablespoons flour

4 eggs, separated, plus 2 extra egg whites

5 ounces goat cheese, such as Boucheron or
    Redwood Hill Farm's Bucheret,
    crumbled

1. Preheat the oven to 375°F. Lightly butter a dish for the soufflé. It needn't be a proper soufflé dish. In fact, I prefer using a 6- to 8-cup round or oval rustic gratin dish. Slowly heat the milk with the aromatics and $\frac{1}{2}$ teaspoon salt in a saucepan. Turn off the heat when it's near a boil and set it aside to steep while you separate the eggs.

2. Melt the butter in a 2-quart saucepan, then stir in the flour. Cook over low heat for a minute, then pour the heated milk into the pan through a strainer and whisk quickly. It should thicken immediately. Cook over low heat, stirring constantly, for 2 minutes, then remove from the heat and stir a little of the hot base into the egg yolks. Next whisk them back into the sauce and stir in the crumbled goat cheese. Taste for salt and season with pepper.

3. Whip the egg whites until they're nearly stiff, then fold them into the base and transfer the whole to the prepared dish. Bake in the center of the oven until puffed and golden but just a little wobbly when you shake the dish, about 25 minutes. Serve immediately, including both the crust from the sides and the "sauce" from the center.

Twice-Baked Soufflé

This method allows you to make individual soufflés hours before you intend to serve them by baking them in a water bath and then reheating them. They will sink after their first baking and look practically hopeless, but once you pour a little cream over the top and send them back to the oven for their second cooking, they will swell magnificently.

This amount will make extra batter, for which you'll need extra ramekins or larger ones. (Or you can make yourself a little hot soufflé for breakfast with the extra.) Otherwise, you might scale the amounts back by a third, using 1 cup milk, 3 tablespoons each flour and butter, 3 eggs and 1 extra white, but the same amount of cheese.

butter and fine, dried bread crumbs for the ramekins

Once-Baked, Regular Soufflé (page 133)

$\frac{1}{3}$ cup light or heavy cream

$\frac{1}{4}$ cup freshly grated Parmesan cheese

1. Preheat the oven to 375°F. Generously butter four 1-cup ramekins, then coat them lightly with bread crumbs, shaking out any excess. Bring a kettle of water to a boil. Make the batter as described in the preceding recipe, then divide it among the ramekins, filling them nearly to the top. Set them in a baking pan, pour in the boiling water to come at least halfway up the sides, and bake in the center of the oven until puffed and golden, about 25 minutes. Remove them and let them stand in the water bath for 10 minutes, then carefully lift them out. They will sink.

2. Slide a flexible spatula around each ramekin to loosen the soufflé, then turn it out. Set it in a lightly buttered individual gratin dish or set them all in a single larger shallow dish, the top facing either up or down. Refrigerate until you need them, but let them come to room temperature while you heat the oven.

3. Heat the oven to 350°F. Spoon the cream over each soufflé, allowing the excess to run down the sides. Cover the top with the grated cheese. Bake until the soufflés have swollen and browned on top, about 20 minutes. Lift them with a flexible spatula to your waiting plates.

Frittata
with sautéed artichokes

Pare, trim, and cook the artichokes first. If you're not planning to cook them right away, cover them with the juice of a lemon and water. Cook them in a nonstick or stainless-steel pan. (Carbon steel and cast iron tend to turn their color.)

The artichokes that grow at the shadowy base of the leaves, called *babies,* have no chokes, so trimming them goes quickly. Once you have the artichokes trimmed and cooked, you can use them three different ways. You can use them to make this frittata, scramble them with the eggs, or make an omelet and fold it over the artichokes. Regardless of their ultimate form, the match of artichokes and eggs is excellent.

Although artichokes are usually problematic with wines, there's no reason to forgo wine here. Try a Grüner Veltliner and see if it doesn't work.

10 baby artichokes

sea salt and freshly ground pepper

6 to 8 eggs

$1/4$ cup chopped parsley or a mixture of tar-
    ragon and parsley

3 tablespoons olive oil

freshly grated Parmesan cheese

1. Preheat the broiler. Snap off the artichoke leaves until you get to the tender yellow-green ones at the center. Slice off the top third and trim the stubs with a paring knife. Thinly slice the artichokes lengthwise into 4 or 5 pieces. Parboil them in salted water for 3 minutes, then pour into a colander and set aside to drain. Whisk the eggs with $1/2$ teaspoon salt and the herbs.

2. Heat 2 tablespoons of the oil in a 10-inch skillet. Add the artichokes and sauté, turning them frequently, until they're golden and tender-firm when poked with the tip of a knife, about 10 minutes. Season with a few pinches of salt and pepper. Tip them onto a plate and wipe out the pan.

3. Add the last tablespoon of oil (or butter if you prefer). When hot, pour in the eggs, then lay the artichokes over the top. Cook over low heat until the eggs are set and light gold on the bottom. Sprinkle Parmesan over the top. Slide the pan under the broiler to finish cooking, then serve.

*hearty
cool-weather
suppers*

Certainly the weather influences what we want to eat, and fall and winter are the times when hearty, filling foods like potatoes, polenta, and rice dishes loom large on the supper horizon. This is not the only time that these ingredients are attractive. There are many lovely summery ways of cooking potatoes (which are new in the summer, in fact), beans, lentils, and rice. However, here they are in their winter aspect—full, filling, and fit for supper.

Of course I'm fully aware that the potato and other carbohydrate-laden foods are today's food pariahs, but I stand by the potato and by all truly whole foods that are unaltered by biotechnology or unnecessary processing. I can't imagine banning all the wonderful varieties of potatoes we have (and all those phytochemicals!) from my kitchen, let alone rice, polenta, stone-ground grits, or sweet potatoes. Do I eat them all the time? No. But sometimes? Definitely!

Knowing that people have conflicting love-hate emotions about starchy foods, I've designed these recipes so that they include a full measure of greens, onions, chiles, beans, and other wholesome foods, in hopes that you will enjoy them fully.

7

Mashed Potatoes and Turnips
with sautéed onions and greens

While mashed potatoes and turnips sounds robust and wintry, this can be a summer dish as much as a winter one.

When your farmers' market offers bunches of sweet little turnips with their greens get two—you can't have too many greens. In winter, when you have storage turnips, use broccoli rabe for the greens. They're closely related in flavor—rabe meaning turnip, in fact.

As for wine, a Sancerre is in order in summer, especially when goat cheese is included in the mash; in fall or winter, a Cabernet Franc from the Loire Valley would be appropriately robust.

4 russet potatoes (about 2 pounds), peeled and chunked	a 3-ounce chunk of goat cheese and/or butter to taste (optional)
3/4 pound or more turnips (8 to 10 small summer turnips)	1 tablespoon butter plus 2 teaspoons olive oil or all olive oil
1 thyme sprig	2 large onions, sliced about 1/4 inch thick
sea salt and freshly ground pepper	1 pound, more or less, turnip greens or broccoli rabe

Begin cooking the potatoes and turnips. While they're cooking, start the onions and the greens. I usually cook the turnip greens in the potato water, but a bunch of broccoli rabe will need more room. If the mash is finished first, keep it warm over a pot of simmering water or in a double boiler. You can also cook the onions and greens ahead of time, then reheat and combine them with the potatoes at the end, making this a somewhat do-ahead dish.

1. Put the potatoes and turnips in a pot, cover with cold water, and add the thyme and 2 teaspoons salt. Bring to a boil and cook, uncovered, until soft, 20 to 25 minutes. Drain, then mash, adding cooking water if needed to thin the vegetables and the cheese and/or butter to taste. Taste for salt and season with pepper. Keep warm in a double boiler if you're not ready to serve.

2. Melt the butter with the oil in a large cast-iron or nonstick skillet. Add the onions and cook over medium-high heat, stirring frequently, until golden and tender, 12 to 15 minutes. Season with salt and pepper and turn off the heat.

3. Lop off the stems of the turnip greens. If using broccoli rabe, peel the thicker stems. Cook in boiling salted water until tender, about 8 minutes in both cases, but taste to make sure. Drain, then add them to the pan with the onions.

4. To serve, mound the mash on a platter and smother it with the onions and greens.

hearty cool-weather suppers

Potato Skillet Pie

Not quite a frittata, not quite mashed potatoes, this hybrid potato pie is nothing if not versatile. By themselves, potatoes are on the neutral side, but they go with practically anything, so you can make extemporaneous variations with ease. You can add a middle layer of sautéed artichokes or garlicky broccoli rabe. Or you can use the dish as a base for a vegetable sauté. Should you have leftovers, slice, brown, and serve them with a tomato sauce or with applesauce and sour cream if you're making a rather unadorned version. Use a well-seasoned cast-iron skillet and your pie will develop a handsome golden crust.

To complete this winter supper, start with crisp green salad and end with something smooth and cool, such as goat milk panna cotta with warm honey. Potatoes, as they are cooked in the basic recipe or the variation with onions, are a welcome match with Pinot Noir. But to play off the artichokes or green garlic in the variations that use them, try a Sauvignon Blanc. If you're including cheese, go with a Zinfandel.

4 tablespoons butter or oil

1 cup bread crumbs or ½ cup grated
  Parmesan cheese for the pan

scant 2 pounds Yellow Finn or Yukon Gold
  potatoes, peeled and chunked

sea salt and freshly ground pepper

2 garlic cloves

4 eggs, lightly beaten with a little water

3 tablespoons chopped sage

1. Preheat the oven to 375°F. Put a 10-inch cast-iron skillet in the oven with a tablespoon of the butter until melted. Brush it around the pan, then scatter bread crumbs or Parmesan cheese into it to make a crust for the potatoes.

2. Put the potatoes in a saucepan and cover with cold water. Add a teaspoon of salt, bring to a boil, then simmer until the potatoes are soft, about 20 minutes. While they're cooking, smash the garlic in a mortar with ½ teaspoon salt until smooth.

3. Drain the potatoes and return them to the pot. Add the garlic and remaining butter and mash. Taste for salt and pepper, making sure the potatoes are highly seasoned. Then stir in the eggs and sage, transfer the mass to the skillet, and smooth the top. Bake until golden and pulling away from the sides of the pan, about 45 minutes. Remove, let stand for 10 minutes, then run a knife around the edge and unmold onto a serving plate.

- *With sautéed artichokes:* Cook the artichokes as described on page 136, seasoning them with tarragon, chervil, rosemary, or another favorite herb. Smooth half the potato mixture into the pan, cover with the artichokes, then cover with the remaining potatoes. Or serve the artichokes alongside the potatoes instead.

- *With fried onions:* Peel and slice 3 or 4 onions. Heat 2 tablespoons butter or olive oil in a large skillet, add the onions, and sauté over high heat until browned around the edges and temptingly fragrant, about 10 minutes. Spoon them over the finished potatoes.

- *With cheese:* Stir 1 to 2 cups grated cheese into the hot potatoes. Consider such cheeses as a sharp aged Cheddar, a nutty Gruyère, goat cheese, Fontina, or, on the lighter end, ricotta, cottage cheese, fromage blanc, or farmer cheese. This is a great opportunity to use up those odds and ends occupying the fridge.

- *With green garlic:* In spring, when the green garlic is available at farmers' markets, peel and mince 3 large heads (it's mild!) along with any tender greens. Simmer them in a little water until soft, then add to the potatoes before baking.

Polenta Squares
with gorgonzola cream, braised greens, and cannellini beans

To me, a truly comforting food is a café au lait bowl of warm polenta lavishly covered with Gorgonzola cheese and toasted bread crumbs. This recipe has the same elements but is less of a curl-up-on-the-couch sort of dish and more something to set the table for and share with company.

The polenta and cheese alone, in smaller portions, make a fine appetizer. But the addition of the braised greens and cannellini beans turns a simple dish into a meal. The richness of the cheese calls for a salad at the end and a clean-flavored dessert, such as a citrus sorbet. But if you love big red wines, the polenta with its cheese presents you with an opportunity to enjoy a full-bodied, rich red Amarone from northern Italy.

Plan to have already made and cooled the polenta so that it's firm and ready to go. If you haven't done that, but you want this for dinner, just serve the polenta soft, on a plate, with the sauce and the vegetables.

Polenta Cooked in the Double Boiler (page 205), cooled until firm
Braised Mixed Greens and Garlicky Beans (page 187)
5 ounces Gorgonzola dolce or Point Reyes blue

1 cup half-and-half or whole milk
2 teaspoons rosemary leaves minced with 1 garlic clove
sea salt and freshly ground pepper
olive oil
semolina or flour for dusting

1. Make the polenta, then turn it into an 8- by 10-inch baking dish. Let it cool until firm or plan to use it in its soft form. Cook the greens and beans.

2. Crumble the cheese into a saucepan and add the half-and-half and the rosemary-garlic mixture. Simmer, stirring, until the cheese has melted. Taste and season with salt and pepper.

3. Film a large skillet with olive oil. Cut the polenta into triangles, dip them in the semolina, then brown on both sides over medium heat. Pile the greens and beans on the plate, add 3 to 4 pieces of polenta, surround with the sauce, and serve.

Greens and Grits

Not those greens—long-cooked mustard and collards doused with pepper sauce—but spanakopita greens—spinach, chard, and dill, seasoned with feta cheese.

My husband, a southerner, reminds me that grits are scary to people outside the South—they think of grits as hot cereal. Think of grits as polenta if you're worried, or substitute polenta. Both, in fact, are grits. Stone-ground grits are best, hands down.

This recipe is vegan if the milk is replaced with water or soy milk and the cheese is omitted. This can stand as a one-dish supper, but you could start dinner with a soup. For wine, put some bubbles in here with a domestic sparkling rosé, such as one from Handley Cellars in Mendocino.

THE GRITS

$1^{1}/_{2}$ cups milk

$1^{1}/_{2}$ cups water

$^{3}/_{4}$ cup stone-ground grits or quick-cooking (not instant) grits

sea salt and freshly ground pepper

butter to taste

THE GREENS

2 small bunches or 1 big bunch of chard, leaves only (12 cups in all)

1 bunch of spinach, leaves only

2 tablespoons olive oil

1 large onion, finely diced

1 bunch of scallions, including half the greens, finely chopped

$^{1}/_{2}$ cup chopped parsley

1 bunch dill, chopped ($^{1}/_{3}$ to $^{1}/_{2}$ cup)

sea salt

$^{1}/_{4}$ pound feta cheese

1. Bring the milk and water to a boil. Whisk in the grits, add $^{1}/_{2}$ teaspoon salt, then lower the heat and simmer, stirring frequently, until the grits taste thoroughly cooked—about 40 minutes for stone-ground, 15 to 20 minutes for quick-cooking (refer to the package).

2. While the grits are cooking, roughly chop the chard and spinach, then wash but don't dry. Heat the oil in a Dutch oven over medium-high heat. Add the onion, scallions, parsley, and dill and cook for about 3 minutes, stirring occasionally. Lower the heat, pile the chard into the pot, and sprinkle with ½ teaspoon salt. When wilted and tender, after 5 minutes or so, add the spinach, cook a few minutes more until tender, then turn off the heat.

3. When the grits are cooked, season them with salt and pepper and add butter. Spoon them onto 4 plates or wide bowls, cover with the greens, crumble the feta over the top, and serve.

Black-Eyed Peas
with coriander and greens

SERVES 4

Chard braised with onions, cilantro, and parsley is one of my favorite dishes, and here it meets up with black-eyed peas. Minus the yogurt, this dish is vegan, but yogurt does complete the proteins.

Serve this earthy, lively mixture with bulgur or rice and a spoonful of creamy yogurt alongside. As Greece is the origin of these flavors, I'd look for spicy Greek red wine, but since Greek wines in general are not easy to find, pour an Italian Rosato from Tuscany such as Castello di Ama or one from Sicily, such as Regaleali.

Frozen black-eyed peas cook in about the same amount of time as the greens, as do dried peas if you use a pressure cooker. While the peas are cooking, start the bulgur, then prep and cook the greens.

1 package frozen black-eyed peas

sea salt and freshly ground pepper

2 tablespoons olive oil

2 big bunches of chard

several handfuls of amaranth, blanched nettles, or wild greens, if available, coarse stems removed

Steamed Bulgur (recipe follows)

1 large onion, finely diced

½ cup chopped cilantro, more or less, with the stems, plus extra for garnish

½ cup chopped parsley or chervil, more or less

2 garlic cloves, finely chopped

1 tablespoon tomato paste

1 teaspoon paprika

yogurt for serving

hearty cool-weather suppers

1. Put the frozen peas in a pot with 3 cups water, $\frac{1}{2}$ teaspoon salt, and a teaspoon of the olive oil. Cover and simmer until tender, about 25 minutes. Meanwhile, chop the chard and any other greens coarsely. Wash but don't dry them. Trim the chard stems, then cut them into fine dice. Start the bulgur.

2. Heat the remaining tablespoon oil in a Dutch oven. Add the onion and cook over medium heat for 5 minutes, stirring frequently. Add the cilantro and parsley to the onion along with the garlic and chard stems. Stir in the tomato paste and paprika, then add the chopped greens. Season with $\frac{1}{2}$ teaspoon salt, give the mixture a stir, then cover tightly and cook over low heat until the greens are meltingly tender, about 25 minutes. They should cook in their own liquid.

3. When the peas are soft, add them to the chard along with their liquid. Taste for salt and season with pepper. Serve with the bulgur, a spoonful of yogurt, and a garnish of fresh cilantro leaves.

Steamed Bulgur

1 cup fine or medium bulgur
sea salt and freshly ground pepper
2$\frac{1}{2}$ cups boiling water

1 tablespoon butter or extra-virgin olive oil,
to taste

Rinse the bulgur, then put it in a bowl with a few pinches of salt and pour on the boiling water. Cover and let stand 15 minutes for fine bulgur, 25 minutes for medium. If there's any excess water, pour the bulgur into a strainer, then heat it with the butter or olive oil. Taste for salt and season with pepper.

Macaroni and Cheese

Everyone loves macaroni and cheese, especially adults, who are surprised to find that it tastes nothing like the stuff they fix for their kids. There are no tricks or exotic elements in this recipe (although I do love including fresh mozzarella for its stretchy strings of warm cheese). Just bake it in a big, gorgeous casserole until it's all crusty and golden. You can set the whole thing up well ahead of time, then bake it when you're ready. Macaroni and cheese makes an easy and enormously satisfying weeknight winter supper for company or family, served with tomato soup and a salad of slivered endive and watercress. In warm weather, I go for a big tossed salad studded with tomatoes, artichoke hearts, chickpeas, and other goodies. A fruit condiment, such as sweet-and-sour quinces with dried fruit or apple-pear chutney, nicely complements the cheese. To drink, have a medium-bodied, fruit-forward Zinfandel, such as Sonoma's Seghesio.

First heat the milk with its aromatics, then let it steep while you cook the noodles. Make the white sauce, combine it with the noodles and cheese, then cover with bread crumbs and bake. Or, if you plan to bake it much later in the day—or even the next day—refrigerate, but allow it to come up to room temperature before baking.

3 cups milk

aromatics: 1 onion slice, 1 bay leaf, 1 garlic clove, 1 small pinch of thyme

1 pound elbow macaroni

3 tablespoons butter

3 tablespoons flour

sea salt and freshly ground pepper

1½ cups grated cheeses: a sharp, aged Cheddar, aged Gruyère, and/or Emmenthal

1 or 2 rounds fresh mozzarella cheese, halved and sliced (optional)

1 cup fresh bread crumbs

1. Rub a 9- by 12-inch casserole with butter. Bring a large pot of salted water to a boil for the macaroni. Preheat the oven to 350°F whenever you're ready to bake. Heat the milk with the aromatics until it bubbles around the edge, then turn off the heat and let it steep for at least 10 minutes.

2. Cook the macaroni in the boiling salted water until al dente and then drain. Rinse with cold water to stop the cooking.

3. Melt the butter in a 3-quart saucepan. Stir in the flour, then pour the hot milk through a strainer all at once into the roux. Whisk briskly until the sauce is thickened, then cook over low heat for 5 minutes, stirring constantly. Season with ½ teaspoon salt and some pepper.

4. Put the macaroni in the baking dish, then pour over the sauce and add the cheese(s). Mix together, even the surface, cover with bread crumbs, and wipe down the sides of the dish. Bake, uncovered, until bubbling throughout and golden on top, 25 to 35 minutes.

hearty cool-weather suppers

Neelam's Festive Rice Pilaf

While the rice is soaking, gather and prepare the rest of the ingredients, make the chile paste, and cook the nuts and dried fruits. Then bring everything together.

Neelam Batra, the author of the prize-winning book *1,000 Indian Recipes,* generously shared this recipe with me. It is a glorious one-pot rice dish loaded with nuts, dried fruits, and vegetables. Neelam suggests serving it with yogurt to which minced fresh ginger, mint, cilantro, and scallions have been added. Without it, the dish is vegan.

A dry Pinot Gris from Alsace has enough fruit to stand up to the spices.

1½ cups basmati rice

6 quarter-size slices peeled fresh ginger

2 large garlic cloves, peeled

1 to 3 fresh serrano chiles, to taste, coarsely
 chopped

3 tablespoons vegetable oil

½ cup shelled raw almonds, coarsely
 chopped

½ cup shelled raw pistachios

¼ cup each raisins, dried cranberries, and
 dried blueberries

1 2-inch cinnamon stick

5 or 6 black cardamom pods, crushed lightly
 to break the skin

1 teaspoon cumin seeds

1 medium onion, thinly sliced

¼ teaspoon ground turmeric

2 cups finely chopped fresh vegetables such
 as carrots, cauliflower, bell peppers of
 mixed colors, summer squashes

½ cup frozen peas

sea salt

½ teaspoon garam masala

1. Wash the rice in 3 or 4 changes of water or until the water runs almost clear. Then soak the rice in 2¾ cups water for about 30 minutes. Using a small spice grinder or food processor, make a fine paste from the ginger, garlic, and serrano chiles.

2. Heat a teaspoon of the oil in a 3-quart saucepan or a skillet large enough to hold the rice. Add the almonds and pistachios and cook over medium heat, stirring, until fragrant and a few shades darker, about 1 minute. Add the dried fruits and cook for another minute. Set aside.

3. Heat the remaining oil in the same pan. Add the cinnamon and cardamom and stir over medium heat for about 1 minute. Add the cumin seeds—they should sizzle on contact with the hot oil—and the onion. Cook, stirring frequently, until golden brown, about 5 minutes. Stir in the ginger-garlic paste and turmeric, then add the vegetables and the peas and cook, stirring, for 2 to 3 minutes.

4. Pour in the rice and its soaking water, add 1 teaspoon salt, and bring to a boil. Reduce the heat to the lowest setting, cover the pan (partially at first until the foam subsides, then snugly), and cook until the rice is done, 10 to 15 minutes. Do not stir the rice while it is cooking.

5. Remove from the heat and lightly fork in the reserved nuts and fruits. Cover the pan and allow the rice to rest for about 5 minutes. Transfer to a serving platter, sprinkle the garam masala on top, and serve.

Green Rice
with roasted green chiles and leeks

A quickly made stock that uses those good leek trimmings adds more flavor to the dish. If you're making this simple stock, start it first, then roast the chiles and chop the leeks. Everything—the rice, chiles, and leeks—cooks together, then the herbs (pureed first) are added at the end, with the sour cream.

"What are you going to make with all those leeks?"

I had to ask. Most people don't buy armfuls of leeks. But my friend's enthusiastic answer—green rice with chiles and leeks—inspired me to go home and make this dish. When I want a little more complexity, I serve this with Mexican oregano, quartered limes, and sliced avocado. But plain is good, too, and leftovers make a terrific rice omelet.

This is a filling weeknight sort of a dish, to which I might add a colorful vegetable for an appetizer, such as vinegared beets nested in their greens or a jícama, orange, and avocado salad. The chile can take away from the earthiness of Old World wines, but a New Zealand Sauvignon Blanc with grassy, herbaceous fruit can stand up to it.

3 cups vegetable stock (see step 1) or water

3 poblano chiles or 4 or 5 Anaheim chiles

1 or 2 tablespoons vegetable oil

1½ cups short- or long-grain rice

6 medium leeks, white parts plus paler greens, chopped (about 3 cups)

sea salt

1 bay leaf

1 cup parsley leaves

½ cup cilantro leaves

1 or 2 ounces Jack cheese, Muenster, or queso fresco, cubed

½ cup sour cream, loosened and stirred with a fork

1. If you're making the stock, put the leek roots and 2 cups of the inner leek greens in a pot with 5 cups water, a grated carrot, a handful of parsley and cilantro stems, a pinch each of dried thyme and oregano, and ½ teaspoon salt. Bring to a boil and simmer, uncovered, for 25 minutes. Strain.

2. Char the chiles over a flame, then drop them into a plastic bag to steam for 15 minutes. Slip off the skins, pull out the seeds, and chop into ½-inch pieces.

3. Heat the oil in a Dutch oven. Add the rice and cook over medium-high heat for about 5 minutes, stirring occasionally. Add the leeks, chiles, 1 teaspoon salt, the bay leaf, and 3 cups stock or water. Give a stir, cook for a few minutes, then lower the heat. Cover and simmer for 20 minutes.

4. While the rice is cooking, puree the parsley and cilantro in a blender with 1 cup water or any extra stock. When the rice is done, stir the puree into it and add the cheese. Swirl in the sour cream just before serving for a pretty white and green effect.

Black Beans
with yellow rice

Make the Coconut Rice (page 107), but instead of setting the rice aside to cool, use the rice hot from the pan, pressing it into a cup first, then unmolding it, or simply scooping in onto the plate and adding the black beans. While you can stop here, pickled pink onions and a wedge of lime make a fetching garnish.

This particular combination of rice and beans is one of my favorites. Conveniently, it's one dish where organic canned black beans do just fine if you take a moment to doctor them up. It's vegan as is.

The sweet red fruit of a Chilean Cabernet or Australian Shiraz would be a lively partner for both the beans and the rice. For dessert, I'd go for something tropical and cooling—a mango sorbet, a basket of pineapple guavas, or a ripe cherimoya.

Coconut Rice (page 107)

2 teaspoons light peanut oil

1 green bell pepper, finely diced

1 small onion, finely diced

1 bay leaf

1/3 cup chopped cilantro, plus leaves for
     garnish

1 garlic clove, minced

1 scant teaspoon toasted and ground cumin
     seeds

1/4 teaspoon chipotle chile, powdered or in
     adobo sauce, or more to taste

2 15-ounce cans black beans with their juice,
     preferably organic (about 3 cups)

1 scant cup coconut milk (or all the coconut
     milk remaining from the rice)

sea salt

2 limes, 1 juiced, 1 cut into 4 wedges

Pickled Onions (page 169), optional

1. Start the rice.

2. Heat the oil in a saucepan. Add the pepper, onion, bay leaf, and cilantro and cook, stirring frequently, for about 5 minutes. Add the garlic, cumin, and chipotle, then the beans and coconut milk. Bring to a boil and simmer until hot. Season with salt and add fresh lime juice to taste.

3. To serve, scoop the hot rice onto a plate or pasta plate. Scoot the beans around the rice and garnish with the cilantro leaves, pickled onions, if using, and lime wedges.

Fragrant Red Lentils
with basmati rice and broccoli romanesco

Start the rice so that it will be ready when the lentils are. Then make the lentils and, while they're cooking, steam the broccoli Romanesco.

These split lentils cook very quickly into a fragrant puree eaten, souplike, with un-adorned basmati rice and, in this instance, the spiraled whorls of bite-sized broccoli Romanesco. (You can vary the vegetable and include such diverse choices as grilled okra, green beans, cauliflower, spinach sautéed in mustard oil, and so forth.)

With the addition of yogurt, whole wheat flatbread, and cheese, such as small por-tions of the Feta and Ricotta Cheese Skillet Pie on page 17 (replace the dill with a salsa verde of diced jalapeños, scallions, mint, cilantro, and lime juice), this supper offers complete protein as well as speed, ease, and succulence. A dry Gewürztraminer, such as Navarro's from Mendocino, will stay with the underlying flavor of the coconut milk with its body and spicy fruit.

Basmati Rice (page 206)

3 tablespoons butter, oil, or ghee

1 small onion, finely chopped

3 teaspoons finely chopped fresh ginger

1 large or 2 medium jalapeño chiles, seeded
   and diced

2 cups split red lentils, rinsed in several
   changes of water

$1\frac{1}{2}$ teaspoons ground turmeric

$\frac{1}{4}$ teaspoon cayenne

1 bay leaf

sea salt

1 can coconut milk

$\frac{1}{3}$ cup finely chopped cilantro, plus sprigs
   for garnish

1 head broccoli Romanesco or cauliflower,
   cut into bite-sized pieces

1 teaspoon mustard seed

$\frac{1}{4}$ cup yogurt

1. Start the rice.

2. Melt 5 teaspoons of the butter in a 3-quart saucepan over medium-high heat. Add the onion, two-thirds of the ginger, and the jalapeño and cook for about 2 minutes. Next add the lentils, 1 teaspoon of the turmeric, half the cayenne, the bay leaf, 3 cups water, and 1 scant teaspoon salt. Bring to a boil, then simmer, partially covered, until the water is absorbed and the lentils are soft, about 15 minutes. Add the coconut milk and simmer for 5 minutes, stirring occasionally. Taste for salt, remove from the heat, and stir in $\frac{1}{4}$ cup of the cilantro.

3. While the lentils are cooking, steam the broccoli pieces until tender but still somewhat firm when pierced with a knife.

4. Melt 2 teaspoons of the butter in a large skillet. Stir in the last of the ginger, turmeric, and cayenne, cook gently over low heat for a minute, then add the vegetables and $1/3$ cup of the cooking water. Raise the heat, add the last of the cilantro, swirl everything around the pan, and cook until the water has evaporated. Season with salt.

5. To finish, heat the remaining 2 teaspoons butter in a small skillet over high heat, add the mustard seed, and cook until it begins to turn grayish, about a minute. Stir this into the lentils.

6. To serve, pack the hot rice into ramekins and turn them upside down, one each, in a shallow pasta bowl. Spoon a cup or more of the lentils around them, then lift off the ramekin, leaving the rice intact. Swirl a few spoonfuls of yogurt into each bowl, then add the broccoli Romanesco. Garnish with big sprigs of cilantro and serve.

Cabbage Parcels
with sweet-and-sour tomato sauce

These little parcels, wrapped in their string, look exceptionally inviting. Both fillings are hearty and they go with the sweet-and-sour tomato sauce. For cabbage, try to find Savoy—the one with crinkly leaves that look like majolica—it's sweet and gorgeous. The dish is vegan if the filling is.

I can't resist including bright orange carrot coins on this colorful plate or starting supper with a carrot soup. A crisp green romaine salad with blue cheese and walnuts might follow, and for dessert a lemon tart or citrus compote. A powerful Alsatian white, such as a Pinot Gris, has balanced fruit for the cabbage's stuffing and enough acidity for the sweet-and-sour sauce.

If you have a filling already made (each roll takes 4 to 5 table-spoons), it doesn't take more than 20 minutes to blanch the cabbage, stuff, and tie these bundles. Start the sauce while you're filling the parcels; then add the parcels and cook. You'll need kitchen string for the packets.

hearty cool-weather suppers

1 green cabbage, preferably Savoy, trimmed
    of any ragged outer leaves

3 to 4 tablespoons sunflower seed or olive oil

4 cups Brown Rice–Mushroom "Burgers"
    filling (page 84) or Feather Fritters
    (page 85)

2 onions, finely diced

1 tablespoon tomato paste

$\frac{1}{4}$ teaspoon ground allspice

1 28-ounce can crushed tomatoes, preferably
    organic

2 tablespoons brown sugar or more to taste

$\frac{1}{2}$ cup dry white wine or the wine you'll be
    drinking

flour for dredging

sea salt and freshly ground pepper

aged red wine vinegar or Chardonnay
    vinegar to taste

1. Cut out a core in the base of the cabbage to make removing the leaves easier. Set a vegetable steamer over boiling water and place the cabbage on top of it. Cover the pan and steam for 5 minutes, then check to see if you can gently pull off the first leaf. If you can't, continue steaming until you can. Remove as many leaves as you can easily, then continue steaming until you can remove more leaves. You'll need a dozen leaves in all. When done, take the cabbage out of the pot to use for something else. Or chop, then steam it and serve it with the cabbage bundles. Stack the leaves with their prettiest sides facing down. Remove any hard cores if they make it hard to fold the leaves.

2. Heat 1 tablespoon oil in a wide nonstick skillet. When hot, add the filling mixture and fry it over medium-high heat, pressing down, turning it occasionally, so that it browns in places. Then place a mound in the center of each leaf and fold to enclose the filling. (If the leaves are very big, use more filling and make fewer of them. If they're so small that they're hard to stuff, overlap two leaves to make one big one. The string will hold them together.) Tie both lengthwise and crosswise with kitchen string to make a little parcel.

3. While you're making the parcels, heat another tablespoon oil in a wide skillet and add the onions, tomato paste, and allspice. Cook over medium-low heat, stirring occasionally, until softened and starting to color, about 15 minutes. Add the tomatoes and sugar along with the wine and 1 cup water. Bring to a simmer.

4. While the sauce is cooking, dip the cabbage parcels in flour, brush off the excess, then brown them lightly in the remaining oil as needed.

5. Taste the sauce for salt and pepper and sharpen it slightly with a few drops of vinegar. Add more allspice if you think it needs it. Arrange the parcels over the sauce, cover the pan, and cook for 25 minutes. Serve with a few tablespoons of the sauce.

hearty cool-weather
suppers

159

light meals for
warm weather

*n*ormally my high altitude ensures a pleasantly warm summer. But while testing the recipes for this book, the entire world heated up to such a degree that I found myself wondering what to cook when it's hot out. There are nights when a gin and tonic and a cucumber salad are my idea of a perfect supper. However, the convention of the meal ultimately takes over, for summer is a great time for eating with friends, late in the evening, when the temperature finally goes from hot to warm.

For this chapter I've chosen dishes that for the most part eliminate the need to turn on the oven or dishes that can be baked in the morning and served later at room temperature, such as the Late-Summer Vegetable Tian on page 176.

Stovetop cooking warms the kitchen far less than an oven, and cooking outdoors is even better—there's a reason summer is grilling season. Platters of grilled vegetables and their sauces can make fine summer fare.

I love warm-weather foods because they are the ones that are so aromatic, colorful, and also likely to come from my garden or the farmers' market. And I like to make enough of something that I can serve it in various ways throughout the week. For example, the Mezze Plates (page 162) provide a home for roasted peppers, grilled eggplant, cold sliced beets, leftover ratatouille, or wedges of a frittata. I also like dishes that are essentially an assemblage of different elements: the Black Bean Tostadas (page 167), with their crisp tortilla, a salad, a little cheese, pickled onions, and some avocado. Diverse and light, it's an ideal summer meal—small but interesting.

Foods that cook quickly are definitely desirable, such as a wedge of golden "fried" cheese (page 166) or pasta with its uncooked sauce of chopped tomatoes (page 171). The garden ragout on page 173 is a good supper dish too, since the chopped ingredients cook quickly, and it needn't be served piping hot.

In addition to the recipes included in this chapter, warm weather calls for the supper sandwiches in the next chapter, tarts, and frittatas, which are usually good at room temperature. Even the Cabbage and Leek Gratin on page 18 is good served cold—just add a little vinaigrette or more of that Mustard Cream. Summer is a great season for vegetable salads, fruit salads, and cooling soups, all of which make fine accompaniments and even light meals in themselves for when it's not merely warm out, but piping hot!

8

Mezze Plates
for a hot night

I've noticed that when I serve an array of simple appetizers in the summer there isn't much interest in dinner afterward. So why not just turn them into dinner? More than once I've put together a mezze spread at a moment's notice, which is how I know that it's easy to do, then watched it disappear over the course of the evening. These particular bites—ideas to work from, really—come from the garden, the pantry, leftovers, and a few very simple recipes. Mix and match your offerings, set them in pretty bowls and arrange them on a table, and serve them with one or more of the good breads we now enjoy in this country, the Golden Grilled or Sautéed Cheese on page 166, or an interesting farmstead cheese or two.

With so many different flavors and dishes, but all of them geared to summer, I'd use this opportunity to open two or three different rosés—from Sicily, Provence, and California.

FROM THE GARDEN

clusters of currant, cherry, and other "fruit" tomatoes

little carrots, scrubbed, with their greens attached

tender, crisp radishes with their leaves, or big Misato rose types, thinly sliced and soaked in ice water until curled, then served with salt and fresh lime juice

summer turnips, thinly sliced, with sea salt

bulb fennel, soaked in cold water, then quartered

lemon cucumbers, cut into wedges

very fresh, new sugar snap peas

melon with freshly cracked pepper

FROM THE PANTRY
AND THE FRIDGE

olives, seasoned with fresh or dried herbs and a bit of orange or lemon zest

roasted peppers drizzled with olive oil

cubes of feta or Manouri cheese (a dense, melt-in-your-mouth Greek cheese similar to ricotta salata), with fresh mint leaves, olive oil, and pepper

roasted almonds or pecans

an American chèvre, such as Humboldt Fog, or a chèvre Camembert

baked ricotta with thyme

Pickled Onions (page 169) or other pickled vegetables

green beans or lentils in an herb vinaigrette

vegetarian suppers

Two New Recipes

Roasted Eggplant
with yogurt

Slash 1 or 2 medium eggplants in several places, fill the gaps with sliced peeled garlic, then bake in a 375°F oven, or at whatever temperature is convenient, until softened, usually about 40 minutes for a 1-pound eggplant. Put in a colander to drain and cool, then scoop out the flesh and mix it with a little yogurt to taste, some minced garlic, chopped mint leaves, sea salt, and freshly ground pepper. Put it in a dish and garnish with mint.

Cold Broccoli Rabe
with lemon

Bring a wide pot of water to a boil. While it's heating, peel the thick stems of the broccoli rabe, then rinse. Salt the water, plunge in the broccoli rabe, and cook until the stems are tender, 5 to 10 minutes, depending on how well done you like your greens. Transfer to a colander and set aside to drain. Put on a platter, drizzle with olive oil, and garnish with lemon wedges.

Mixed Grilled Vegetables
with two sauces

A platter of grilled vegetables becomes an immensely appealing dinner option on a hot day. There's a reason we grill in the summer. Although a fire is hot, it's outdoors; the heat goes into the sky instead of the kitchen. This collection is offered with two sauces— a rusty Romesco and a green chimichurri sauce. In addition to the vegetables, you can grill Halloumi cheese (page 166), for a truly mixed grill. As is, the dish is vegan.

You might want to start the meal with chilled tomato soup, gazpacho, or sliced melons with pepper. While vegetables are not big protein sources, the Romesco sauce is, with its almonds and hazelnuts, which leads right to our wine, a Spanish Rosato from the Navarra region, such as Chivite's Gran Fuedo.

4 leeks, white parts only, halved lengthwise and steamed until tender

3 or more fennel bulbs, cut into slabs and steamed until tender

olive oil as needed

sea salt

5 red bell peppers, 2 whole, 3 halved, seeded, pressed to flatten

3 golden peppers or cubanelles, halved, seeded, and pressed to flatten

6 Japanese eggplants, halved lengthwise and scored

6 fresh onions, halved or cut into 1-inch rounds and secured with a toothpick

6 medium zucchini, halved lengthwise and scored, if smallish, or cut into $^{1}/_{2}$-inch slabs if large

Romesco Sauce (page 198)

Chimichurri Sauce (page 198)

1. Start with the vegetables that need precooking—the leeks and the fennel—and steam them until tender-firm. Brush with olive oil and season with salt.

2. Grill the whole red peppers while the grill is hottest, char them, then put them in a covered bowl to steam. Set them aside to use in the Romesco sauce. Brush the flattened peppers with oil and grill, blistering but not charring the skins. They should look as if the peppers are tender and the skins have just loosened.

3. Brush everything else with oil and season with salt, then place on the grill. If you want grill marks, let them stay in one spot for 5 to 8 minutes or so before turning them 45 degrees. Cook on both sides until each vegetable is done, then remove to a platter and arrange attractively, garnishing with blossoming herbs or even squash blossoms. Make the sauces and serve them with the vegetables.

It takes patient engagement to grill vegetables. Don't try to rush them or use too hot a fire—burned vegetables aren't the equivalent of rib ends. But grill plenty. Having leftover grilled vegetables is a huge bonus in the summer kitchen. They make great impromptu salads and sandwich fillings, you can do a million things with grilled peppers, and grilled anything adds character to a vegetable soup. Following are just some suggestions. Both of the sauces can be made ahead and refrigerated. In fact I've suggested them as accompaniments for other dishes in this book, and they're great to have on hand.

light meals for warm weather

Golden Grilled or Sautéed Cheese

Halloumi is the cheese you can grill—it says so right on the package—and you can sauté it too. You can also sauté queso blanco, a mild Mexican cheese that's delicious with the salsa of roasted tomatoes and garlic on page 118. Both cheeses turn soft, color beautifully, and hold their shape. The Halloumi is a bit salty, like feta, but denser, and it squeaks when you eat it. Queso blanco is milder, and both are as close to being an instant meal of real food as you're likely to get. Halloumi keeps for a long time, so keep a pack on hand along with your aseptic boxes of tofu for one of those nights when you need to eat *now.*

Although it's very satisfying and filling, you won't be eating a big portion, so the rest of the meal is especially important. Anything that isn't creamy or based on cheese would go here. Any number of chilled soups and vegetables salads would round out supper, such as a chilled melon or tomato soup, a lentil salad, or several small vegetable salads. Consider something to hold the cheese—a flatbread, tortilla, or seeded cracker—and varied accompaniments such as seasoned olives, roasted peppers, grilled pepper and chile strips (rajas), or corn. For wine, a neutrally oaked Chardonnay, such as a Pouilly-Fuissé, would cover all these bases in a refreshing and noncompetitive manner.

½ pound queso blanco or Halloumi cheese
olive oil

Slice the cheese lengthwise into 4 pieces, each about ½ inch thick. Heat a nonstick skillet and brush it with a little olive oil. Add the cheese and cook until golden, 3 to 4 minutes, then turn and cook the other side. Serve immediately with any of the suggested sides or with a cool vegetable salad.

Sides and accompaniments

- Peel a cucumber, then keep paring off the flesh, down to the seeds, making long, thin strips. Toss them with a little salt, lemon, and fresh dill and pile them on the plate.
- Make a salad of finely diced cucumber, peppers, celery, fennel, scallions, and dill. Toss it with olive oil, add a squeeze of lemon, and serve it with the cheese.

- Chop cold cooked broccoli rabe or spinach and season it with a squeeze of fresh lemon juice. Or serve it with the Sautéed Heirloom Tomatoes on page 170.
- In winter "fried" cheese is very good served with stewed lentils covered with crisped bread crumbs and chopped parsley. In summer, the lentils can become a salad.
- Drizzle over the hot cheese Salsa Ranchera (page 118) or another lively sauce, such as the Chimichurri or the Romesco Sauce on page 198.

Black Bean Tostadas
with slivered cabbage, avocado, and pickled onions

MAKES A LIGHT MEAL FOR 4

Two small corn tortillas with their toppings are just the right size for a meal, which is to say not too big. A good choice for a casual hot-weather supper, these tostadas can be enjoyed by vegans who use soy-based sour cream and cheese substitutes.

I'd start this meal with a fresh corn soup, garnished with strips of poblano chile or seasoned with tomatoes and basil. (Corn soups are always good served on the tepid side.) I'd end with a guava-based dessert—a feijoa Bavarian cream, for example—or a strawberry and passion fruit sorbet. An Australian Shiraz would be a fine match with the tostadas, and a Sémillon/Chardonnay, also from Australia, with the corn soup.

These tostadas are far easier to throw together than providing a recipe suggests, for all the little parts are indeed very simple. Start with the pickled onions, then make the beans, salad, tortillas, and guacamole or salsa.

THE BEANS

Pickled Onions (page 169)

2 teaspoons light olive or vegetable oil

$^1/_4$ cup finely diced onion

$1^1/_2$ teaspoons dried epazote or 1 tablespoon fresh

1 garlic clove, minced

1 15-ounce can black beans, preferably organic

sea salt

6 cups finely sliced green cabbage

sea salt

¼ cup finely diced white onion or scallion

2 pinches of dried oregano

2 tablespoons chopped cilantro

⅓ cup white wine vinegar or lime juice

⅓ cup boiling water

8 small corn tortillas

oil

2 small avocados, peeled and sliced or made into guacamole

1 jalapeño chile, seeded if desired, then diced or sliced into rounds

crumbled queso fresco or feta cheese

½ cup sour cream, thinned with a little milk

4 lime wedges

cilantro sprigs for garnish

Salsa Cruda, without the avocado (page 118)

1. Make the pickled onions and let them stand while you get everything else ready.

2. Heat the oil in an 8-inch nonstick skillet and add the chopped onion and epazote. Cook over medium-low heat, stirring frequently, until the onion starts to brown, 3 to 4 minutes, then add the garlic and cook for 1 minute more.

3. Add a third of the beans with their juices, raise the heat a little, and mash them until fairly smooth. Add the rest of the beans and cook, scraping up the simmering beans and mashing them until they're somewhat thickened but still a tad soupy. They'll thicken as they cool in any case. Season with salt and keep them warm.

4. Toss the cabbage with a few pinches of salt and the onion. Add the rest of the salad ingredients, toss well, and refrigerate until ready to use.

5. Heat a large skillet or griddle. Brush the tortillas with oil. Lay them on the hot skillet and cook on both sides until crisp and golden. Or bake in a 400°F oven until crisp, 6 to 8 minutes.

6. Put 2 tortillas on each plate and spread the warm beans over each. Mound the cabbage on top, add the avocado, jalapeño, cheese, a drizzle of sour cream, and the pickled onions. Put the lime wedges on the side and garnish with a few sprigs of cilantro. Pass salsa at the table.

Pickled Onions

1 small red onion, thinly sliced into rounds

sea salt

1 teaspoon sugar

apple cider vinegar or rice wine vinegar

Toss the onion rounds with a pinch of salt and the sugar. Put them in a bowl with vinegar to cover; they'll turn bright pink in about 15 minutes, and will keep for about 5 days in the refrigerator.

Sautéed Heirloom Tomatoes
on garlic-rubbed toast

Have your tomatoes marinating an hour ahead of time, or just before, if that's what works best. Make the toast, heat the tomatoes, put them together, and you're done.

Here's a tasty little supper for listless eaters on a hot night. For tomatoes I pick what's in my garden, which is likely to be a mixture of ripe red Sweet 100s, orange Sun Golds, Green Zebras, and a yellow heirloom or two. These briefly cooked tomatoes, caught just at the moment between fresh and stewed, make an excellent addition to countless summer dishes. This recipe is vegan.

You might flesh out this meal by starting with a chilled soup. It could be a yogurt soup with rice and spinach or a tomato soup (stay with tomatoes if they're good). Add a simple salad and a few nibbles, such as roasted almonds, and end with a glorious fig tart. Chianti Classico and other simple northern Italian reds like Dolcetto from the Piedmont or Valpolicella from Verona are classic with tomatoes. If you prefer a white, try a New World Sauvignon Blanc, especially if you add the capers.

2 heaping cups sliced, quartered, or diced tomatoes, assorted kinds and colors	1 tablespoon olive oil
	sea salt and freshly ground pepper
1 shallot, finely diced	2 large pieces ciabatta, semolina, or other
1 large garlic clove, ½ minced	rustic bread
3 basil leaves, slivered	a few drops of balsamic vinegar

1. Toss the tomatoes with the shallot, minced garlic, basil, olive oil, and a pinch of salt. Set aside until you're ready to eat.

2. Grill or toast the bread. Rub it with the other ½ clove of garlic.

3. Heat a medium skillet. When hot, add the tomatoes. Swirl the pan around to warm them through, add a few drops balsamic vinegar and some pepper, then spoon onto the toast and serve. They should just warm up and release their juices, not fall apart.

Variations

- Spread ricotta thickly over the toast, season with salt and pepper, drizzle with oil, and warm it in a toaster oven before adding the tomatoes.
- Sear thin slices of tofu (page 95), deglaze the pan with balsamic vinegar, then put on toast and cover with the tomatoes.
- Spoon the tomatoes over ravioli.
- Serve them with the Ricotta Omelet on page 124 or the Zucchini Skillet Cakes on page 82.

Hot Pasta
with fresh tomatoes

Here is a pasta that I make regularly from August until the end of the first hard freeze in October. It is the lightest, most perfumed summer pasta I know—and vegan. You can enjoy it hot or warm.

Because our season is short, I grow the small (that is, quick to ripen) "fruit" varieties of tomatoes—cherry, plum, currant, and pear, as well as peach and Sun Golds. They're sweet and gorgeous. I use them as they ripen, all the different kinds and colors at once. But it doesn't matter what kind of tomato you use as long as it's been grown in good soil, in the sun, and truly ripened on the vine. As for the pasta, use a shape to catch all the good sauces, such as shells or "gnocchi," which resemble the dumplings by the same name. A simple refreshing, fruity, and lively wine is called for here, such as a Vernaccia from Tuscany or a Pinot Grigio from Alto Adige.

3 cups cherry-type tomatoes, halved or
    quartered
1 shallot, finely diced
1 garlic clove, minced
3 tablespoons best olive oil or more to taste
2 tablespoons salt capers, soaked in water
    and drained, or brined capers, rinsed

$1/3$ cup pitted Niçoise olives
6 basil leaves, torn or slivered
sea salt and freshly ground pepper
$1/2$ pound gnocchi-shaped pasta
a few drops of balsamic vinegar (optional)

1. Bring a pot of water to a boil for the pasta. Meanwhile, put the tomatoes in a roomy bowl with the shallot, garlic, olive oil, capers, olives, and basil. Season with a little salt and some pepper.

2. When the water is boiling, add salt and cook the pasta. Drain the pasta, shake off the excess water, add it hot to the tomatoes, and toss. Taste for salt, add pepper and a few drops of vinegar if you like, and serve.

While you're heating water for the pasta, prepare the tomatoes. Then cook the pasta, add it hot to the bowl, and toss.

Variations
Possible additions:
- More garlic
- Toasted pine nuts
- Marjoram instead of basil, or chopped parsley, or purple basil for garnish
- Fresh mozzarella cheese, diced
- Big heirloom tomatoes, peeled first, the seeds strained from the juice, the flesh chopped

light meals for warm weather

Summer Potatoes
stewed with eggplant, peppers, and olives

Begin with the eggplant if you want to salt it; it should sit for at least 20 minutes. (If you're using really fresh eggplant, and I hope you are, you won't have to do this.) Cook the onions, potatoes, and peppers over plenty of heat to sear them a bit while the eggplant is browning, then combine the two, add the remaining ingredients, and simmer until done.

This is one of those accommodating dishes that can be timed to fit *your* schedule. The potatoes can be tender in 25 minutes, or you can cook the stew much longer. I once left the house thinking the stove was off, and when I returned to my slow-simmering stew 4 hours later I found that the flavors were amazingly rich, the textures surprisingly intact. Look for big cubanelles or smaller pimientos and use them instead of, or with, the bell peppers. For potatoes, you'll want new, yellow-fleshed fingerlings. While fresh tomatoes are my preference, they often lag behind the eggplant in season, so in their place I use canned. If you're inclined to add them, this is the kind of dish that can easily include chickpeas or cooked white beans. In any case, this dish is vegan.

I'd serve this dish with a spinach and tomato salad to start, have a plum kuchen for dessert, and a fruity Sonoma Zinfandel or a spicy Provençal red wine to drink.

3 or 4 long Asian-type eggplants
  ($1\frac{1}{2}$ pounds or more)
sea salt and freshly ground pepper
3 tablespoons olive oil
1 onion, thickly sliced
1 pound fingerling potatoes, scrubbed and
  sliced lengthwise

2 large bell peppers, red and yellow if
  possible, cut into $\frac{1}{2}$-inch strips
2 pounds fresh tomatoes, diced, or 1 cup
  canned in sauce
1 large garlic clove, chopped with a handful
  of parsley leaves
$\frac{1}{3}$ cup black olives, pitted

1. Remove strips of skin from the eggplant to give it a striped effect, then slice it diagonally about $\frac{3}{4}$ inch thick. Toss with salt and set aside for 20 minutes or longer. Rinse and pat dry. Heat half the oil in a wide skillet, add the eggplant, and turn it right away. Cook over medium heat until golden on the bottom, then turn and cook the second side, about 10 minutes. It needn't cook through—just take on some color.

2. While the eggplant is browning, heat the rest of the oil in a Dutch oven. When hot, add the onion, potatoes, and peppers. Cook over high heat, stirring occasionally, until browned here and there, 6 to 8 minutes. Lower the heat, season with 1 teaspoon salt, and pepper to taste. Then stir in the tomatoes and all but a tablespoon or so of the parsley-garlic mixture. (If you've used canned tomatoes with their sauce, add a cup or so of water so that the stew is not too thick.)

3. Add the eggplant and olives and gently mix everything together. Cover, reduce the heat to low, and cook slowly until the potatoes are tender, about 25 minutes, or longer if time allows, to concentrate the flavor. Serve garnished with the remaining parsley and garlic.

Garden Ragout for Midsummer
with marjoram pesto

This ragout, which is nearly a soup, allows you to use all the great vegetables from the summer garden—the new garlic and delicate white turnips, the summer squash, skinny green beans, sweet onions, and ripe tomatoes. It doesn't heat up the kitchen—you're cooking for only about 15 minutes—and with only two of this and three of that, the preparation goes quickly. It's especially nice if you have your own home-cooked beans, so that their broth becomes the cooking liquid. This recipe is vegan.

Start supper with an array of crostini and end with a salad and a cheese plate. You'll want a good rustic bread for dipping. I'd like a ripe nectarine for dessert, and to drink, a fruity Dolcetto from the Piedmont.

Cut all the vegetables first. The pieces needn't be even, but make them small—$^1/_2$-inch cubes for the quick-cooking squash, half that size for the carrots, and midway for everything else. While they're cooking, make the sauce.

1 shiny new onion (as opposed to an old storage onion) or 2 leeks (the white parts and an inch of the pale greens), finely diced

2 medium zucchini, green or yellow, cut into $^1/_2$-inch or smaller dice

2 to 3 medium carrots (about 6 ounces), cut into small dice

3 small white turnips, peeled if desired and finely diced

4 white mushrooms, caps closed, diced into $^1/_2$-inch chunks

a handful of green beans, tipped, tailed, and cut into 1-inch pieces

2 tablespoons olive oil

3 garlic cloves, slivered

sea salt and freshly ground pepper

a few basil or marjoram leaves

Marjoram Pesto (recipe follows)

1 cup cooked flageolet or white beans, plus their broth (see page 208)

1 large ripe tomato or a dozen cherry tomatoes, halved, quartered, or diced

*light meals for
warm weather*

1. Cut all the vegetables, then warm the oil in a wide, deep pot. Add the vegetables (minus the cooked beans and tomatoes), plus half the garlic. Raise the heat and cook, stirring frequently, just to warm them up. Season with ½ teaspoon salt, a bit of pepper, and add 2 cups bean broth or water. Bring everything to a simmer or slow boil, slip a few basil or marjoram leaves into the pot, then lay a piece of parchment paper directly over the vegetables so that those on top don't dry out.

2. Make the pesto.

3. After 10 minutes, stir the beans into the pot with a cup of their broth. Add the tomatoes and cook for 5 minutes more or until the vegetables are done. Ladle the vegetables into soup or pasta plates, add a generous spoonful of the pesto to each, and serve hot or warm.

Marjoram Pesto

1 small slice country bread, crusts trimmed

2 tablespoons aged red wine vinegar or more to taste

1 garlic clove, coarsely chopped

sea salt and freshly ground pepper

¼ cup marjoram leaves

3 tablespoons capers, drained if brined, soaked in water if salt cured

½ cup pine nuts

1 cup finely chopped parsley

⅓ to 1/2 cup extra-virgin olive oil, as needed

1. Soak the bread in 2 tablespoons vinegar.

2. Pound the garlic with ½ teaspoon salt in a mortar until smooth, then work in the marjoram, capers, pine nuts, and parsley until you have a coarse puree. Add the vinegar-soaked bread and ⅓ cup olive oil and work until the sauce is well amalgamated. Season with pepper and taste for vinegar, adding a little more if you think it needs it. Add oil (or water) to thin the sauce slightly.

Late-Summer Vegetable Tian
of slowly roasted peppers and onions

Begin by cooking the
onion-pepper base.
While it's cooking,
thinly slice the
vegetables, then arrange
them over the top.

While a tian is usually the intended side dish for grilled meats, it makes a delectable vegetarian main course for those who don't require huge amounts for dinner, or who are happy to get them at the periphery instead of the center. The key to goodness starts with getting your hands on vegetables from your farmers' market, then slicing them thinly and baking them very slowly. This can be done in the morning while it's cool. The dish is vegan as is.

This tian begs for good bread—a great crispy-crusted baguette, ciabatta, or perhaps a focaccia you've made yourself. Cannellini beans seasoned with no more than floral olive oil, sea salt, pepper, and a fleck of parsley would make a fine side dish. For a sauce, try a simple salsa verde—parsley with lemon, some pine nuts, and olive oil—or a lemon mayonnaise seasoned with a few cloves of pounded garlic. Drink an aromatic white wine, such as Vernaccia. Staying in the wine region, finish with a glass of Vin Santo, biscotti, and fruit.

$^{1}/_{4}$ cup olive oil

3 bell peppers, preferably red, orange, or
    yellow, thinly sliced

1 large onion, such as a torpedo onion, thinly
    sliced

2 bay leaves

6 thyme or lemon thyme sprigs

sea salt and freshly ground pepper

1 teaspoon tomato paste

$^{1}/_{2}$ cup dry white wine

6 plum tomatoes, yellow, red, or both

2 to 3 small oblong eggplants, bands of skin
    removed, sliced $^{1}/_{4}$ inch thick

$2^{1}/_{2}$ cups thin rounds of yellow and green
    zucchini

2 plump garlic cloves, slivered

$^{1}/_{4}$ lemon, thinly sliced

1. Preheat the oven to 325°F. Oil a shallow earthenware gratin dish. Heat 2 tablespoons of the oil in a wide skillet, then add the peppers, onion, bay leaves, and 2 thyme sprigs. Season with $^{1}/_{2}$ teaspoon salt and a little pepper and cook gently over medium heat until the vegetables are tender and the onion is starting to brown at the edges, about 15 minutes. Work in the tomato paste, then deglaze with the wine, letting it cook away until a syrupy sauce remains. Spread the mixture in the oiled dish.

2. Drop the tomatoes two at a time into a small pot of boiling water for 15 seconds or so, then drop them into a bowl of cool water. Slip off the skins, then slice them into rounds.

3. Arrange the sliced tomatoes, eggplant, and zucchini over the pepper mixture, overlapping them either carefully or haphazardly, making a fairly uniform layer in either case. Tuck the remaining thyme sprigs, slivered garlic, and lemon slices among the vegetables, season with salt and pepper, then drizzle the remaining olive oil over all.

4. Cover tightly with foil and bake for 1 hour and 45 minutes. Remove the foil and continue baking until everything is very tender. Serve warm or later in the day at room temperature.

Yellow Peppers
stuffed with quinoa, corn, and feta cheese

SERVES 4

Stuffed peppers may sound like winter fare, but it's summer when peppers and corn are at their peak, and with this light, pretty filling, these peppers are absolutely appropriate for hot weather.

Seasoned with cilantro, chiles, and cumin, and studded with corn and spinach, the quinoa is so compellingly good that you might just want to dive in and forget the peppers altogether. The peppers do, however, frame the quinoa in such a way as to give it the focus a main dish needs, and they look very pretty sitting on their bed of red onions. Omit the feta and these peppers are vegan.

I like these peppers with black beans (page 208) or a black bean soup and maybe some chard, even though there's spinach in the filling. For dessert, I'd go for a soothing cinnamon ice milk with nut cookies or a plate of sliced melons. A New World Riesling, such as Bonny Doon Pacific Rim Riesling, would be the wine to quaff with this meal.

sea salt and freshly ground pepper

1 cup quinoa, rinsed well several times

3 tablespoons olive oil

1 bunch of scallions, including 2 inches of the greens, thinly sliced into rounds

2 jalapeño chiles, finely diced, seeded if desired

1 garlic clove, finely chopped

1 teaspoon ground cumin

2 cups, more or less, fresh or frozen corn kernels (from 3 ears corn)

1 bunch of spinach, leaves only, or $\frac{1}{2}$ pound spinach leaves

$\frac{1}{2}$ cup chopped cilantro

$\frac{1}{4}$ pound feta cheese, cut into small cubes

2 large red onions, thinly sliced into rounds

$\frac{1}{2}$ cup white wine (can be Riesling)

4 yellow and/or orange bell peppers

1. Bring 2 cups of water to a boil. Add $\frac{1}{2}$ teaspoon salt, then the quinoa. Give it a stir, then cover and simmer over low heat until the grains are tender and reveal their spiraled germ, about 15 minutes.

2. Warm half the oil in a wide skillet. Add the scallions and chiles, cook over medium heat for about 2 minutes, then add the garlic, cumin, corn, and spinach, along with 2 tablespoons water. When the spinach is wilted, add the cilantro, quinoa, and feta. Toss everything together, taste for salt, and season with pepper.

3. Heat a tablespoon of oil in a wide skillet. When hot, add the onions and sauté, stirring frequently, until they start to color around the edges, after several minutes. Pour in the wine and deglaze the pan, giving the onions a stir as you do so. Season with salt and pepper and distribute in a baking dish (or two) large enough to hold the peppers.

4. Slice the peppers in half lengthwise without removing the tops or stems, then cut out the membranes and seeds. Simmer them in salted water until tender to the touch of a knife but not overly soft, 4 to 5 minutes, and remove. Fill them with the quinoa and set them in the baking dish(es).

5. Preheat the oven to 400°F. Drizzle the rest of the oil over the peppers and bake the peppers until heated through, 20 to 30 minutes, then switch the heat to broil and brown the tops. Serve hot, warm, or at room temperature.

*supper
sandwiches*

*a*ll the good rustic breads that are being made across the country these days really come into play here. In fact, it's largely their goodness and strength that elevate the sandwich to supper status.

While a sandwich may sound like the ultimate informal supper meal, I use the term rather loosely. For me, a supper sandwich is more likely to consist of a slice of these rustic breads, toasted, then covered with something as fine as asparagus and Fontina cheese or as rustic as lentils cooked in red wine. In fact, most of these sandwiches are truly knife-and-fork foods. They make quick, satisfying little suppers, whether you're eating that meal early in the evening or at night after a movie or a long day at the office. And a supper sandwich can easily be a meal in itself, though of course you can always heat up some soup, throw together some small appetizers, and of course, pour a glass of wine.

I've resisted the temptation to include those ever-homey and satisfying numbers like Welsh Rarebit and cheese toasts here. But I do find that very thinly sliced cheese laid over hot toast and again over a vegetable, be it broccoli rabe or asparagus, gives a sandwich the robustness and roundness that it needs to become supper. But then I am very fond of the complex flavors of cheeses and the way they interact with vegetables. It's my culinary habit, I suppose. If it's not yours, by all means leave out the cheese.

9

Asparagus and Leeks
on toast

Here is a vegetable-intense supper—good toast smothered with a stew of tender new asparagus with spring leeks, green garlic, and young spinach—the result of a spring farmers' market visit. If you've only got asparagus and leeks to cook with, do so. If there are peas or fava beans around, include them, too. If there isn't any green garlic, well, so be it. Omit the cheese, use olive oil instead of butter, and the dish is vegan.

An Australian Sémillon or even a simple fruity red wine, such as a Cabernet Franc from the Loire Valley, served slightly chilled, can stand up to the asparagus.

Only the tips and first 5 inches of the asparagus are used, so plan to use the remainder, plus any of your vegetable trimmings, to make a delicious soup stock. Soak the asparagus tips while you prep everything else, then cook the vegetables and make the toast.

1½ pounds asparagus, the top 5 inches or so, peeled if thick

5 teaspoons butter

2 skinny leeks, white parts only, thinly sliced into rounds and rinsed

1 or 2 small heads of green garlic, peeled and finely diced

sea salt and freshly ground pepper

4 handfuls of young spinach leaves

fresh lemon juice or white wine vinegar to taste

3 slices whole wheat levain or country bread

thinly sliced Italian Fontina cheese

1. Soak the asparagus for 5 minutes or so to dislodge any sand that might be hiding in the tips, then give it a rinse.

2. Melt 1 tablespoon of the butter in a medium skillet. Add the leeks and green garlic, stir to coat well, cook for a minute or so, then add ½ cup water or a splash of white wine and cook over medium-low heat for about 3 minutes. Add the asparagus, season with ½ teaspoon salt, and add another ½ cup water. Simmer until the asparagus is tender, about 8 minutes, adding water as needed in small increments so that you're left with about ½ cup pan juices.

3. Add the spinach and the last bit of butter. Raise the heat a little and cook until the spinach is wilted. Taste for salt, season with pepper, and add a few drops of lemon juice to sharpen the flavors.

4. Toast the bread, then cover with the thin slices of cheese. Slice each piece in half diagonally and arrange 3 pieces on 2 plates. Spoon the vegetables over all, along with their juices, and serve.

*supper
sandwiches*

Roasted Portobello Sandwich
with mozzarella and braised cooking greens

Look for mixes of young, sweet braising greens—small chard leaves, kale, amaranth, and spinach. They have lots of character and are often tender enough to be sautéed in short order. Of course, sautéed spinach is always good with mushrooms, too. (I'd use two bunches for four people.) Toast—or an English muffin—serves as a raft for your mushroom.

The earthiness of a Pinot Noir is classic with mushrooms. The extra cool-climate acidity in a Pinot Noir from Oregon—a Ponzi Pinot Noir from the Willamette Valley—would be a good complement. See the first variation that follows for a substantial vegan version.

4 large portobello mushrooms

2 tablespoons olive oil, more or less

2 garlic cloves, chopped with a small handful of parsley leaves

sea salt and freshly ground pepper

¾ pound small braising greens, trimmed and washed, or 2 bunches of spinach, stems removed, leaves well washed

2 pinches of hot red pepper flakes

4 slices bread, such as ciabatta, or 4 English muffins

2 4-ounce balls fresh or smoked mozzarella cheese, sliced and set on paper towels to drain

1. Preheat the oven to 400°F. Remove the stems from the mushrooms, wipe off the caps, and then scrape out the gills with a spoon. Drizzle the inside of the caps with half the oil and sprinkle on all but a teaspoon of the chopped garlic and the parsley. Season with a few pinches of salt and some pepper, then transfer to a shallow baking pan and bake until the mushrooms are hot and starting to sizzle, 8 to 10 minutes.

2. Heat the remaining oil in a skillet; add the greens and sauté with the reserved parsley-garlic mixture and pepper flakes to wilt. Season with salt. If the greens need more cooking, add a few tablespoons water to the pan and cook until tender. Cook off all the liquid before adding the greens to the mushrooms.

3. Toast the bread or muffins. Divide the cheese among the mushroom caps, cover with the greens, and bake until the cheese is soft and warm, 5 to 7 minutes. Remove and set each mushroom on its waiting toast and serve.

- For a lusty vegan version, omit the mozzarella and replace it with Skillet-Seared Tofu (page 95).
- In summer, slice large, ripe tomatoes into rounds ½ inch thick and set them over the soft cheese.
- Spread a thin layer of olive paste over the muffins or toast.
- Instead of bread, cut firm polenta into rounds, set the mushrooms with their cheese over the top, and heat in a 400°F oven until melted. Remove and smother with the hot greens.
- For a very succulent handheld sandwich, put these mushrooms and their greens (plus olive paste and tomatoes) between 2 slices of toast or bread.

Broccoli Rabe on Toast
with tapenade and goat's milk gouda

I could eat broccoli rabe three times a week, not only with pasta but this way—forked over a big slab of toasted country bread, covered with olive paste and a thin shaving of cheese. If goat Gouda doesn't appeal, try aged Gruyère cheese, Italian Fontina, or Sonoma Dry Jack cheese. For wine, a young Pinot Noir from Santa Barbara or a simple Pinot from Burgundy's Côte Chalonnaise would be good. A Provençal-style red or rosé wine is another choice that gives a nod to the olives. Without the cheese, this is vegan.

1 hefty bunch of broccoli rabe with small, tight buds	a few pinches of hot red pepper flakes
sea salt	2 or 3 large slices country bread
2 tablespoons olive oil	about $\frac{1}{3}$ cup olive paste or Tapenade (page 199)
1 garlic clove, chopped	thinly sliced, goat's milk Gouda

1. While you heat several quarts of water for the broccoli rabe, peel the larger stems. When the water is boiling, add salt and the greens. Cook until the stems are tender, about 5 minutes, then scoop the greens into a bowl, holding back a cup of the cooking water. Chop them coarsely.

2. Warm the 2 tablespoons olive oil in a wide skillet over medium heat. Add the garlic and pepper flakes, then the cooked broccoli rabe with $\frac{1}{2}$ cup or so of the reserved water so that there will be plentiful juice. Cook until it's sufficiently tender and hot. Taste for salt.

3. Toast the bread, spread with tapenade and lay the cheese on top. Set the bread on plates, then smother it with the greens, including a spoonful of the juices. Shave a little more cheese over the top and serve.

Braised Mixed Greens
and garlicky beans on toast

When a friend dropped by unexpectedly for dinner, I could see that there wouldn't be enough of the greens I was cooking. I added some cooked cannellini beans to the pan, and now they're a must.

You can play with this combination. Imagine braised spinach with flageolet beans (a delicate version), wild spinach with pinto beans (a southwestern version), or broccoli rabe with Romano beans (Roman in spirit). Any mixture of greens can be spooned over garlic-rubbed toast, pasta, and polenta. (See the polenta with Gorgonzola on page 145 for example.) For wine, try a Spanish red, such as a Grenache-based Priorat wine or a Spanish white Albariño. Without the Parmesan, this is vegan.

Start with the onion. Wash and chop the greens, then add them, wet, to the pan. Make the toast once the greens have cooked.

1 tablespoon olive oil, plus extra for finishing

1 small onion, finely diced

2 plump garlic cloves, 1 slivered, 1 halved

1 pound greens, such as chard mixed with the tips and leaves of broccoli rabe or a mix of small braising greens, washed and chopped

a few leaves or a few handfuls of sorrel, 5 or 6 lovage leaves, or a handful each of chopped cilantro and parsley (optional)

sea salt and freshly ground pepper

1½ cups cooked beans (borlotti, cannellini, etc.), home-cooked or canned

3 to 4 slices chewy country bread

shaved Parmesan cheese or crumbled Gorgonzola

1. Heat the oil in a large skillet or Dutch oven. Add the onion and cook over medium-high heat, stirring occasionally. Once the onion starts to soften a bit, after 3 to 4 minutes, add the slivered garlic. Cook for a minute more, then add the greens and any herbs. Season with ½ teaspoon salt.

2. As the greens cook down, turn them in the pan to bring the ones on top closer to the heat. Once they've all collapsed, add ½ cup water or bean broth, lower the heat, and cook, partially covered, until tender. Depending on the greens you've chosen, this could take as little as a few minutes or as long as 20. Just make sure there's some liquid in the pan, for in the end you'll want a little sauce. When the greens are done, add the beans, heat them through, then taste for salt and season with pepper.

3. Toast the bread and rub it with the halved garlic. Arrange on plates and spoon on the greens and beans. Drizzle with olive oil. Garnish with the cheese and serve.

supper sandwiches

187

Thin Herb Omelet and Arugula Sandwich

Any frittata can be made thin and tucked into a sandwich, but these herb-flecked omelets, tucked into whole wheat pita breads with arugula, are appealing in the spring, when the first delicious eggs, the first fresh herbs, and arugula are coming into the farmers' market. For accompaniments, you might serve sautéed snow peas with pea greens or asparagus braised with peas and spring onions and an apple-rhubarb pandowdy for dessert. A young Chianti Classico, a normale rather than a riserva, would be a good weekday choice with this simple meal.

5 eggs

sea salt and freshly ground pepper

4 thin scallions, including an inch or more of the greens, thinly sliced

2 tablespoons chopped parsley

2 teaspoons chopped tarragon

2 teaspoons minced chives

olive oil or butter

freshly grated Parmesan cheese

2 to 4 whole wheat pita breads, sliced horizontally

mayonnaise

a handful of arugula leaves

1. Whisk the eggs with a few pinches of salt, a few grindings of pepper, and a tablespoon of water. Add the scallions and herbs.

2. Heat an 8-inch nonstick skillet with a teaspoon of olive oil or butter. Ladle in a quarter of the egg mixture and swirl it around the pan. Lower the heat. Grate a little cheese over the surface. When the eggs are set, turn them over with a spatula and briefly cook the second side. Slide the finished omelet onto a plate and repeat with the rest of the eggs.

3. Spread one side of half of the pita bread with the mayonnaise, add an omelet and the arugula, top with the second piece of bread, and serve.

Grilled Cheese Sandwich
with tapenade

No matter what you call it—a panino or a grilled cheese sandwich—there's nothing quite as yummy as the combination of warm, soft cheese, crisp toast, and a thin layer of tapenade. My latest favorite cheese is Carmody, a Teleme-like cheese from Bellwether Farms in California that oozes with ease over the toasted bread. Of course all kinds of cheese are wonderful in a grilled cheese sandwich—fresh or smoked mozzarella, Gorgonzola, goat cheeses, Fontina, Robiola, and Cheddar, to name but a few. Serve this with a chopped vegetable salad and you have a great little supper, one to enjoy with a choice of wines—a lovely Beaujolais, a Provençal rosé, or a California Vin Gris, such as Bonny Doon's Le Cigare Volant.

2 slices whole wheat country bread or rustic
    Italian bread
Tapenade (page 199) to taste

Carmody or Teleme cheese, sliced
butter or olive oil for the bread

1. Cover one slice of bread with a thin swipe of olive paste, then add the cheese. Top with the second slice of bread and lightly butter it or brush it with olive oil.

2. Set the sandwich buttered side down in a frying pan and butter the top of the second piece. Cover and cook over medium-low heat until crisp and golden. Turn and cook the second side. Take your time and go slowly so that the cheese melts without the bread's burning. There's no need to weight the sandwich.

Variations

- Add beefsteak tomatoes or slow-roasted tomatoes to the sandwich.
- Open the finished sandwich and smother the cheese with sautéed onions.
- Try Cheddar on rye bread, with onions or tomatoes.
- Grilled Fontina cheese with several fried sage leaves set on top is really good.
- For cheese, use queso blanco. When done, open the sandwich and spoon Tomatillo Salsa (page 201) or Chimichurri Sauce (page 198) over the cheese.
- Try grilled manchego cheese between slices of bread that have been spread first with Romesco Sauce (page 198).

Spinach Quesadillas

MAKES 2 LARGE
QUESADILLAS, SERVING
2 TO 3

Cook the greens, get your condiments together, such as guacamole or pico di gallo, then make your quesadillas.

I know people who are addicted to the spinach quesadillas served at Santa Fe's Ramblin' Café, including me. They are packed full of spinach, with just enough cheese and chile to round out its flavor and hold it all together.

In the spring I make a version using quelites, or wild spinach, a New Mexican wild green in the goosefoot family, which has a much greener, earthier taste. Both quelites and spinach are so filling that three wedges of a single quesadilla may well be enough. At lunch I drink iced tea, but for dinner I'd go for a rosé, such as Ojai Vineyard's Vin Gris. It would be refreshing, and it can stand up to the salsa served alongside.

1 tablespoon olive oil or vegetable oil

1 small onion, finely diced

1 red or green jalapeño chile, seeded and diced

a good pinch of dried Mexican oregano or several pinches of epazote

½ pound spinach leaves, without stems, washed (about 8 cups)

sea salt

½ cup chopped cilantro

4 whole wheat tortillas

⅓ cup grated Muenster cheese, Jack, or queso blanco

Salsa Cruda with Avocado (page 118)

sour cream (optional)

1. Heat the oil in a wide skillet and add the onion, chile, and oregano. Cook over medium heat until the onion is translucent, about 4 minutes, then add the spinach. Sprinkle with a few pinches of salt and cook until wilted and tender, about 4 minutes longer, adding a little water to the pan if it dries out. Stir in the cilantro. Taste for salt. If the spinach seems excessively wet, pop it into a strainer and press the excess moisture out.

2. Using 2 skillets, warm one tortilla in each, flipping them over so that both sides get hot. Scatter the cheese over the hot surface, then cover with spinach and a second tortilla. Cook over medium heat until the bottom tortillas are a little crisp, then flip the quesadillas over and cook the second side. Slide the finished quesadilla onto a cutting board, cut into quarters, and overlap them, 3 to 4 wedges on a plate. Serve with salsa and a dollop of sour cream if desired.

Grilled Vegetable Sandwich or Wrap
with chipotle mayonnaise

Make the chipotle mayonnaise first and set it aside. Grill the vegetables, then put the sandwich together.

Here's a spicy, juicy sandwich that you can play with in various ways. In addition to—or instead of—the given vegetables, you can include grilled eggplant or crookneck squash. You can put a slice of Monterey Jack cheese in the middle or use vegan mayonnaise and vegan cheese. You can even add grilled tofu. But for bread, use a soft roll or wrap everything in a large wheat tortilla.

If it's not convenient to grill outdoors, use a ridged cast-iron stovetop pan. It's a great tool, especially if you're making only one or two sandwiches. With the spicy mayonnaise, make margaritas or serve beer, iced tea, or fresh limeade.

$1/3$ cup mayonnaise

pureed canned chipotle chile packed in adobo or chipotle chile powder to taste

$1/2$ fresh lime

2 6-ounce zucchini, cut lengthwise into slabs about $3/8$ inch thick

1 large red or yellow bell pepper, halved lengthwise and flattened

1 large onion, cut into rounds about $3/8$ inch thick

1 long green New Mexican or Anaheim chile per person

olive oil for the vegetables

sea salt

2 long rolls or 2 large tortillas

2 slices Monterey Jack or Muenster cheese (optional)

1 ripe tomato, sliced

lettuce

1. Stir together the mayonnaise, $3/8$ teaspoon chipotle chile, and the juice of the $1/2$ lime, then set aside while you grill the vegetables. Wait at least a few minutes before tasting and adding more chile—it takes a little time for the heat to blossom.

2. Brush the vegetables lightly with olive oil. Heat a ridged cast-iron pan or outdoor grill. Slowly cook the zucchini, peppers, onion, and chile, turning them at 45-degree angles for grill marks and on both sides. The peppers and chiles needn't be charred—just softened, as the skins will be left on. Season everything with salt.

3. Spread a roll with the mayonnaise. Layer over the vegetables and add the sliced cheese if using. Add tomato slices and a leaf of lettuce, then the top half of the roll. Press down, slice in two, and enjoy. Or spread a large wheat tortilla with the mayonnaise, add the lettuce and vegetables, and roll to make a wrap.

Wine-Braised Lentils
over toast with spinach and red pearl onions

This may not be usual fare, but lentils over toast make a delicious winter supper, especially when they've been cooked in wine. Butter is very good with lentils, so use some to finish them before serving. Or use walnut oil, which is not only delicious but makes the dish vegan.

Serve with a medium-bodied red wine with balanced fruit, acidity, and earthiness. A Barbera from the Piedmont or a Crozes-Hermitage from the Rhône would make a good match for the earthy lentils.

Cook the lentils first. Prepare the greens and the onions while the lentils are cooking, combine them at the end, and serve.

¾ cup French green (Le Puy) or black (Beluga) lentils, cleaned and rinsed

4 teaspoons olive oil

⅓ cup each diced onion, carrot, and celery

2 garlic cloves, 1 crushed, 1 halved

1 tablespoon tomato paste

1½ cups dry red wine

1 teaspoon prepared Dijon-style mustard

sea salt and freshly ground pepper

12 red pearl onions

1 big bunch of spinach or other greens, such as Tuscan kale, leaves only, washed

1 tablespoon butter or walnut oil, or to taste

4 slices sturdy country bread

1. Parboil the lentils for 5 minutes and drain.

2. Heat 1 tablespoon of the oil in a 2- or 3-quart saucepan. Add the diced vegetables and cook over medium-high heat for several minutes, browning them a bit. Add the crushed garlic, mash the tomato paste into the vegetables, then pour in the wine and stir in the mustard. Add 1½ cups water, the drained lentils, and 1 teaspoon salt. Simmer, covered, until the lentils are tender, 30 to 40 minutes.

3. While the lentils are cooking, blanch the pearl onions in boiling water for 1 minute, then drain. Peel off the skin, then put them in a pan with the rest of the olive oil and cook over medium heat, sliding them in the pan now and then, until tender and beginning to color, about 5 minutes. Add a splash of wine or water toward the end and deglaze the pan. Season with salt and pepper.

4. Wilt the spinach in a skillet in the water clinging to its leaves. Season with salt and pepper. (Tuscan kale will take about 7 minutes.) Stir the cooked greens into the lentils, add a tablespoon of butter or the walnut oil, taste again, and season to taste.

5. Toast the bread and rub it with the halved garlic. Cut each piece in thirds and arrange them on the plates. Spoon the lentils over the toast and garnish with the onions.

basics

condiments and sauces

When the main thing you're cooking for supper is simple to a fault, a sparkling condiment or pungent sauce will carry the day. Black beans and rice become so much more when you add scarlet pickled onions and a spoonful of guacamole to the plate. A big, bold Romesco sauce does wonders for a platter of grilled vegetables, as does harissa, and both work wonders on a sandwich. A scrambled egg in a tortilla becomes far more than a stop-gap measure when you add a robust salsa ranchera or a lively salsa cruda. Gorgonzola sauce with polenta and greens? Delicious! Same with anything that calls for a tomato sauce when that sauce is your own.

The effort spent on a sauce or a condiment can allow you to streamline the rest of your menu. These are not difficult or even particularly time-consuming to make, and many of them will keep for days, if not weeks, in the refrigerator.

Guacamole

Guacamole should be a little chunky, never puree-smooth.

2 tablespoons finely diced white onion or
    scallion, including some of the green

2 tablespoons chopped cilantro

1 serrano or jalapeño chile, finely diced

sea salt

2 avocados

1 tomato, seeded and finely diced

fresh lime juice to taste

Grind or chop the onion, cilantro, and chile with $\frac{1}{4}$ teaspoon salt to make a paste. Peel and mash the avocado with a fork. Add the onion mixture and the tomato to the avocado and season with lime juice and salt to taste. If you're not serving the guacamole right away, press a piece of plastic wrap directly onto the surface to keep it from browning.

Romesco Sauce

This has long been one of my favorite sauces. Especially good with grilled vegetables, spread it over grilled bread in a sandwich. It's great to have a bowl on hand and it will keep, refrigerated, for a week or so.

1 slice country-style bread

½ cup almonds or hazelnuts or a mixture

3 garlic cloves

1½ teaspoons ground red chile or hot paprika

4 Roma tomatoes, roughly chopped

2 tablespoons chopped parsley

1 teaspoon sweet paprika

2 charred red bell peppers, peeled and seeded

¼ cup sherry vinegar

½ cup olive oil

sea salt

Grill or toast the bread until golden and crisp, then grind it with the nuts and garlic in a food processor. Add everything but the vinegar and oil and process until smooth. With the machine running, gradually pour in the vinegar, then the oil. Taste and make sure the sauce has plenty of piquancy and enough salt.

Chimichurri Sauce

This Latin American sauce is also good on grilled foods, whether meats or summer vegetables. It depends more on freshness for its success, so plan to make it and use it the same day.

1 cup parsley leaves or a mixture of parsley and cilantro

3 garlic cloves, peeled and chopped

½ cup olive oil

1 to 2 tablespoons sherry vinegar or fresh lemon juice, to taste

sea salt and freshly ground pepper

several pinches of hot red pepper flakes

Put the parsley and garlic in a food processor and pulse to make a rough paste. Add the oil, the vinegar, starting with a tablespoon, $^1/_2$ teaspoon salt, plenty of black pepper, and the pepper flakes and puree. Taste to make sure there's enough vinegar, then refrigerate in a covered jar until needed.

Harissa

MAKES ABOUT $^1/_2$ CUP

This Tunisian condiment makes scrambled eggs, a sandwich, or a bowl of chickpeas truly exciting. It will keep for weeks, refrigerated.

6 dried red New Mexican chile pods

1 or 2 guajillo chiles or additional New
   Mexican chiles

2 plump garlic cloves, coarsely chopped

sea salt

1$^1/_2$ teaspoons caraway seeds

1 teaspoon each cumin and coriander seeds

1 tablespoon olive oil, plus extra for storage

Wipe off the chiles with a damp cloth, discard any gray or yellowed areas on the skin, then tear them into pieces, shaking out the seeds as you do so. Discard the seeds and stems. Cover the chiles with boiling water and let stand for at least 30 minutes to soften. Drain. Puree the chile with the garlic, $^1/_4$ teaspoon salt, the spices, and oil in a small food processor until smooth. Pack into a clean jar, cover the surface with oil, and refrigerate.

Tapenade

MAKES 1 CUP

1 cup pitted Niçoise or Gaeta olives

2 tablespoons capers, rinsed, or salt capers,
   rinsed first, then soaked (see page 214)

2 garlic cloves, minced

grated zest of $^1/_2$ large lemon and fresh
   lemon juice to taste

3 tablespoons finely chopped parsley

plenty of freshly ground pepper

4 to 6 tablespoons olive oil

basics

Pound the olives, capers, garlic, lemon zest, 1 teaspoon lemon juice, the parsley, and pepper in a mortar or food processor, leaving a little texture. Stir in the olive oil so that the tapenade is loose enough to spread easily. Taste for lemon juice and add more, if needed.

Peanut Sauce

Fresh and green, this peanut sauce is thin in texture but big on flavor. It's particularly good with tofu and tempeh, over brown rice or Asian noodles.

$1/2$ cup raw peanuts

1 tablespoon roasted peanut oil or regular peanut oil

$1/2$ cup chopped cilantro

1 tablespoon chopped mint leaves

zest and juice of 2 limes

2 garlic cloves

$1/4$ teaspoon chipotle chile powder or 1 serrano chile, chopped

sea salt to taste

1 teaspoon soy sauce

Toast the peanuts in the oil in a skillet over medium-low heat until golden and fragrant, about 5 minutes. (If your pan is too hot and they're browning too rapidly, take the pan off the heat and leave them until golden.) Put the peanuts with their oil in a food processor with the remaining ingredients and pulse until smooth, adding up to $1/2$ cup water to thin the sauce. Taste for salt and soy sauce.

Tomatillo Salsa

This tart, lively Mexican salsa is always good with eggs and dishes that include a lot of corn.

8 plump tomatillos, husks removed

2 serrano or jalapeño chiles

1 small onion, chopped

1 plump garlic clove, coarsely chopped

1/2 cup coarsely chopped cilantro leaves

1 epazote sprig, if available

sea salt

Put the tomatillos, whole chiles, and onion in a small pan of boiling water. Simmer until the tomatillos turn a dull green, after 4 to 5 minutes, then scoop everything out and puree in a blender with the garlic, cilantro, and epazote. Season with salt to taste.

Warm Goat Cheese Sauce

This makes a glorious finish for vegetable ragouts, crêpes, and roasted vegetables, and it couldn't be easier to make.

3/4 cup soft goat cheese

1 cup milk or half-and-half

1 garlic clove, smashed in a mortar with

   1/2 teaspoon sea salt

sea salt and freshly ground white pepper

2 teaspoons minced rosemary, basil, or thyme

Put the cheese, milk, and crushed garlic in a medium skillet or saucepan, and simmer over medium heat, stirring, to melt the cheese. (The longer you cook the sauce, the thicker it will be.) Taste for salt, season with pepper, then stir in the herbs.

Make the sauce using Gorgonzola in place of the goat cheese, light or heavy cream, and rosemary for the herb. Serve it with polenta or over a baked potato or roasted beets. Of course, it's delicious over pasta.

Warm Gorgonzola Sauce

basics

Take advantage of ripe tomatoes that are cracked, sun-blistered, and available at a good price to make tomato sauces to freeze for later use. A food mill separates the skins and seeds from the pulp in minutes. If you don't have a food mill, you'll have to peel, seed, and dice the tomatoes before cooking them, so you can see that this inexpensive tool can save a lot of time and effort.

MAKES 2 CUPS

Fast, Fresh Tomato Sauce

Finish this sauce with a little olive oil and use it as is or use it to build a more complex sauce. For example, you could cook some minced onion or shallot in olive oil with rosemary (or parsley, basil, or oregano) and garlic, then add the tomato sauce and simmer for 20 minutes. You could finish it with a spoonful of cream or sharpen it with a few drops of aged balsamic vinegar.

2½ pounds ripe tomatoes, preferably plum types, such as Roma or San Marzano, coarsely chopped if you have a food mill, peeled, seeded, and chopped if you don't

1 plump shallot or ½ small onion, finely diced

1 garlic clove, slivered

sea salt and freshly ground pepper

1 tablespoon olive oil or more to taste

Put the tomatoes in a heavy pan with the shallot and garlic. Cover and cook over medium-high heat. The tomatoes should yield their juices right away, but keep an eye on the pan and add a few tablespoons of water if it becomes dry. Once the tomatoes have thoroughly broken down, after about 20 minutes, pass them through a food mill to get rid of the skins and seeds. Return the pot to the stove and cook over low heat, stirring frequently, until it's as thick as you want. Season with salt and pepper to taste and stir in the oil.

Long-Cooked Tomato Sauce

When my Italian teacher lifted the lid off her pan of tomato sauce that had been simmering for hours, I was surprised by its deep fragrance and color. It was a good reminder of the virtues of a long-simmered sauce. Rather than adding sugar to correct acidity, she simmers her sauce with a whole, peeled carrot that does the same thing, but in a better way. For tomatoes, paste types, of course, have the most meat and least juice, but I've had no problems using a mix of varieties.

4 to 5 pounds fresh tomatoes, rinsed	sea salt
¼ cup olive oil	1 bay leaf
½ cup finely diced onion	1 thyme sprig
½ cup finely diced celery	1 basil sprig
1 whole peeled carrot	

1. Put the tomatoes in a stainless-steel Dutch oven, with a lid. Turn on the heat and press down on a few of the tomatoes. They should start giving up their juice right away. Cover and cook over medium heat until they have burst their skins and are broken apart, about 20 minutes. Pass them through a food mill to extract the skins and seeds. Don't worry if the sauce looks thin.

2. Rinse out the pot, turn on the heat, and add the oil. When hot, add the diced vegetables and sauté over medium-high heat for several minutes, or until the onion has softened. Add the whole carrot, tomato puree, ½ teaspoon salt, and the herbs. Simmer over low heat, stirring occasionally, until the sauce has thickened as much as you wish. Taste and finish seasoning with salt to taste. Remove the carrot before using.

Five-Minute Tomato Sauce
using canned tomatoes

It's true. You can have a tomato sauce based on canned tomatoes—the tomato of choice for a good part of the year—in a very few minutes. Start with diced canned tomatoes, or if you prefer a smoother sauce, crushed tomatoes. Simmer them in a garlic-scented olive oil for 5 minutes, and you're there.

1 tablespoon olive oil

1 garlic clove, peeled and crushed

1 15-ounce can diced or crushed tomatoes

good pinch of dried marjoram or oregano

1 teaspoon tomato paste

sea salt and freshly ground pepper

Heat the oil in a small skillet with the garlic. When you can smell the garlic, add the tomatoes with their juices and the herb, crushed between your fingers. Cook over a lively heat, smashing the tomatoes against the pan to break up the larger chunks. Stir in the tomato paste to fortify the flavor. Taste for salt—it may not need any—and season with pepper.

polenta, rice, and beans

Polenta
cooked in the double boiler

This recipe produces a soft polenta without requiring much of your attention. It does, however, take over an hour, since it cooks slowly in a double boiler.

Polenta is like mashed potatoes in that it can absorb huge amounts of delicious fat. I leave it to you to add whatever enrichments you like and in the quantities you desire.

1 quart water	1 tablespoon butter, to taste
1½ teaspoons sea salt	1 cup freshly grated Parmesan cheese
1 cup coarse cornmeal, preferably stone-ground	(optional)

Bring a few inches of water to a boil in the lower half of a double boiler, then lower the heat. Bring the quart of water to a boil in the top of the double boiler, placed directly over the heat. Add the salt and whisk in the cornmeal. Cook, stirring constantly, until the consistency is smooth, after several minutes, then set the pan over the simmering water and cover. Cook, giving it a stir every 20 minutes or so, until tender and cooked through, about 1¼ hours. Check now and then to make sure there's ample water in the bottom of the double boiler. Just before serving, stir in the butter as desired and the cheese, if using.

Basmati Rice

Rinse 1 cup of basmati rice gently and well in several changes of water, swishing it about with your fingers. Drain, then put it in a saucepan with 2 cups water and $\frac{1}{4}$ teaspoon sea salt. Bring to a boil, then turn the heat to very low, cover the pan, and cook for 16 minutes. Turn off the heat and let it stand 5 more minutes before fluffing with a fork and serving.

Saffron Rice

If you use short-grain risotto or paella rice, this will be dense, whereas long-grain rice ends up lighter, with more separate grains.

4 teaspoons butter or oil	$\frac{1}{3}$ cup dry white wine
$\frac{1}{2}$ cup finely diced onion	2 cups boiling water
2 pinches of saffron threads	sea salt
1 cup rice (short-, medium-, or long-grain)	1 small bay leaf

Melt the butter in a wide saucepan, then add the onion and saffron. Cook over medium heat, stirring frequently, until the onion has softened and the saffron has stained it golden, about 5 minutes. Add the rice and give it a stir, then pour in the wine and let it cook away. Add the water, $\frac{1}{2}$ teaspoon salt, and the bay leaf. Reduce the heat to low, cover the pot, and cook until the rice is done, 15 to 18 minutes. Gently fork apart the grains, then serve.

Black Rice

This earthy-tasting rice, sometimes referred to as Chinese "forbidden" rice, gets its black color—and longer cooking time—from the black layer of bran that is still attached to each grain. Soaking the grains before cooking them makes a more tender rice.

> $1^{1}/_{2}$ cups black rice
> sea salt

Wash the rice in several changes of water, running your fingers through the grains, then tipping off the liquid. Pour off all the water, then put the rice in a pot and cover it with $2^{3}/_{4}$ cups water. Soak for an hour, then add a scant teaspoon salt and bring to a boil. Turn the heat to low, cover, and cook for 35 minutes. Turn off the heat and let the rice stand for 10 minutes to steam before removing the lid. (If you don't have time to soak the rice, cook it in 3 cups water for 40 minutes instead of 35.)

Wild Rice

Real wild rice is not as glossy and black as the hybridized varieties, but it has a more delicate and complex flavor. It is not easy to find outside of Minnesota, Wisconsin, and environs, but when you do find it, cook it like this. (This method can be used for all wild rice, regardless of how wild it really is.) You can get the real thing through the mail from The White Earth Land Recovery Project at www.nativeharvest.com.

> 1 cup wild rice, swished around in several   sea salt and freshly ground pepper
>   changes of water   butter or oil to taste

Put the washed rice in a pot with plenty of water to cover and $1/_{2}$ teaspoon salt. Bring the water to a boil, then lower the heat, cover the pot, and cook at a simmer until some of the grains have begun to burst and all are starting to become tender, about 30 minutes.

basics

The time will vary with the rice used. Turn off the heat, pour off the water, and return the pot to the stove. Cover it tightly and let stand for the grains to steam and finish cooking, about 15 minutes. Gently fork the grains apart and serve, seasoned with butter or oil, salt to taste, and pepper.

Beans

MAKES 2½ TO 3 CUPS

Cooking your own beans is hardly difficult—it just requires working around the time they need. One approach is to cook them overnight in a Crock-Pot. Another, the one I rely on regularly, is to start with unsoaked beans and cook them in a pressure cooker, which takes 25 to 35 minutes in all, depending on the type of beans used, their age, and the hardness of the water. Or you can simply simmer them in water with aromatics, whether or not they've been soaked first.

You might as well double this recipe, then freeze leftovers in 1-cup portions so that you have them on hand when you need them. Home-cooked beans will always have the best texture and flavor. Plus their cooking liquid is a valuable asset as a stock.

1 cup dried beans, picked over, rinsed, and
    soaked, either overnight or for 1 hour in
    freshly boiled water to cover
2 bay leaves
1 small onion, quartered

several parsley sprigs
1 large garlic clove, sliced
1 teaspoon olive oil
sea salt

If you soaked the beans, drain them, cover them with 6 cups fresh water, and bring to a boil. Otherwise, rinse the beans and cover them with 2 quarts water. Boil, uncovered, for 10 minutes, skimming off any foam that collects. Lower the heat, add the remaining ingredients except the salt, cover, and simmer until the beans are partially tender, 30 minutes to 1 hour, then add 1 to 2 teaspoons salt, to taste, and continue cooking until the beans are tender but not mushy. Let them cool in their broth. Remove the aromatics and discard them. Pour off the broth and reserve it for stock. The beans can now be used wherever they're called for.

stocks and seasonings

Mushroom Stock

1/2 cup dried porcini mushrooms

2 teaspoons olive oil

1 onion, coarsely chopped

1 carrot, chopped

1 large garlic clove, sliced

2 mushrooms, sliced, plus any trimmings

2 teaspoons tomato paste

1 tablespoon fresh marjoram or 1 teaspoon dried

1/2 cup dry white or red wine

1 tablespoon flour

salt and freshly ground pepper

1. Cover the dried mushrooms with 3 cups hot water and set aside.

2. Heat the oil in a saucepan over high heat. Add the onion, carrot, garlic, and fresh mushrooms and their trimmings. Sauté, stirring occasionally, until well browned, about 10 minutes.

3. Reduce the heat to medium, stir in the tomato paste, marjoram, and wine, and sprinkle on the flour. Once the wine has reduced to a syrupy consistency, after about 3 minutes, add the porcini, their soaking water, 1/2 teaspoon salt, and a little pepper. Simmer for 20 minutes, then strain. The stock can be frozen.

Porcini Powder

This fragrant powder gives you a way to add all that good mushroom flavor to a dish without having to make a stock. You can, of course, do this with other dried mushrooms as well, but these have the most flavor. Simply take a small handful of dried porcini mushrooms and grind them in a spice mill until fine. Store the powder in a jar with a tight-fitting lid and use it to season sauces, soups, and vegetable dishes of all kinds.

MAKES 1 QUART

Stock for Stir-Fries

If you make a lot of stir-fries, keep some of this stock to have on hand to replace the ½ cup or so of chicken stock that is usually called for in stir-fries. It will keep, refrigerated, for at least a week. If you don't use it that quickly, make half the quantity or plan to freeze what you don't use.

5 dried Chinese black or shiitake mushrooms

1 bunch of scallions, including the greens

1 small onion or leek, the white part plus the pale greens, finely sliced

2 large carrots, thinly sliced

1 cup mung bean sprouts

½ cup chopped cilantro stems and leaves

2 slices fresh ginger, chopped

3 garlic cloves, chopped

1 6-inch piece kombu (dried kelp)

1 tablespoon light soy sauce or mushroom soy sauce

1 tablespoon mirin

1½ teaspoons salt

1 teaspoon roasted sesame oil

Put all the ingredients in a pot except the sesame oil. Add 6 cups cold water. Bring to a boil and cook at a lively simmer for 40 minutes. After 20 minutes, remove the mushrooms and set them aside to use in a stir-fry or miso soup. Strain the stock and return to the stove. Add the oil and taste for salt and soy sauce, adding more to taste if needed.

Canned Beans

I've never been a fan, but now there are some organic canned beans that are free from the off-flavor that used to be so prevalent. Even the liquid is usable. The main problem with canned beans is that they're too soft, turning mushy when cooked. The good thing, of course, is that they're terribly convenient. Still, it's your own home-cooked beans that will be best. They're obviously not a last-minute endeavor, but once you have a pot made, you can freeze them in 1- or 2-cup portions so they're ready and waiting for you. See page 208 for how to cook beans.

Bouillon Cubes and Premade Stocks

When you look at chefs' recipes for vegetable stocks, they do look wonderful, and they should be, based as they are on luxurious quantities of leeks and celery root, handfuls of shallots and wild mushrooms, bundles of fresh herbs, and so forth. Shopping in a restaurant walk-in makes such full-flavored stocks possible. But a home cook who tosses those ingredients in a shopping basket will get quite a shock at the checkout counter. We're easily talking about $25 stocks! It's one thing if you have unlimited funds or a garden, but an expensive proposition if you don't. So what about those bouillon cubes and commercial stocks?

I've wanted to like them, but I don't. There's always a dominant acrid flavor that takes over, so in the end I'd rather use water. However, there is an Italian porcini bouillon cube (Star brand) that really does convey the flavor of porcini without the intrusion of false notes. Like all bouillon cubes, it is very salty, so you have to use it with care, tasting as you go. As for aseptic packages of vegetable stock, I can't say I'm wildly excited about them or that they add a great deal to a dish. The boxed mushroom stocks fare better, but you can do wonders with some porcini powder on hand (see page 210)—a truly big seasoning that takes no more effort than grinding a dried mushroom in a spice mill.

Other Canned Foods

Mostly this means tomatoes. The season for fresh is very short—two months, maybe a little longer—so for much of the year I keep organic canned tomatoes in various forms (Muir Glen is the brand) on hand. They're not only organic, but they're delicious as well and hands down better than any cottony so-called fresh tomato from the supermarket.

Dairy: Milk and Cheese

When it comes to milk, I would hope that you use organic so that it isn't laced with drugs and antibiotics, rBGH, or traces of GMO grains. But whether it comes from a cow or a soybean, whether it's skim, low fat, or whole, pasteurized or not, the choice is yours.

As for cheeses, I look for raw-milk cheeses, which taste much better—they're more alive—and cheeses made by small, hands-on producers. Excellent raw-milk cheeses are available today, including many that are being made here in the United States. They are indeed very special, but also quite costly, so I prefer to offer them as a cheese course rather than use them for cooking.

To learn more about raw-milk cheeses and American farmstead cheeses, go to slowfoodusa.org or turn to Laura Werlin's handsome and informative *The All American Cheese and Wine Book*.

Nondairy Dairy

Although I don't specify it, vegans will choose butter and cheese, yogurt, and sour cream made from soybeans or rice instead of the same made from milk. These products simulate true dairy products, although they taste and can behave differently.

Eggs

I always use organic eggs from free-range chickens. I trust their quality and their taste is much better than that of eggs from battery layers. The chickens are happier as well.

Frozen Foods

I have, in a fairly diligent manner, tried many of the prepared frozen foods that are available at natural food stores and have found them to be appalling, which is why I am still committed to cooking at home and pretty much from scratch.

When I'm testing recipes out of season, which of course is bound to happen, I sometimes have to turn to frozen vegetables, and I've also found them disappointing. Baby artichokes are never well pared, and they have an unpleasant citric-acid aftertaste.

Frozen spinach is stemmy and takes longer to cook than fresh, and corn is generally starchy and dull tasting.

But some of the organic products that are now available, such as those made by Cascadian Farm, are pretty good. Its frozen corn is surprisingly fresh tasting and sweet, as are its peas, and the spinach isn't that stemmy after all. Although I am devoted to eating fresh and local foods—and blessed with the opportunity to do so—I do turn to these organic frozen vegetables now and then, for they can save the day. And I admit it: I love having a bag of edamame or black-eyed peas on hand to cook at will.

Mushrooms, Dried and Fresh

Fortunately, these are readily available at gourmet stores and natural food stores, and if you travel to Italy, it's always well worthwhile to pick up an extra bag at the airport when you're leaving. Porcini raise the quality of any mushroom dish in which they're used. As with all dried mushrooms, they need to be soaked in hot water for at least 30 minutes before being used, longer if you have time. By all means use the soaking water, pouring it first through a very-fine-mesh sieve to strain out any forest dirt. They're expensive, but if you aren't buying fresh porcini or other wild mushrooms, they will give you that special wild flavor. (See Mushroom Stock and Porcini Powder, pages 209 and 210.) I find that until you get into shiitake or the truly wild mushrooms, button, brown, cremini (baby bellas), and portobellos pretty much taste alike, which is to say, mushroomy but not wildly so. Except for the interesting and diverse shapes the larger mushrooms offer, they aren't always worth the extra cost, which is sometimes double. I'd rather spend the money on dried wild mushrooms, hydrate them, then use them with their liquid to flavor whatever mushrooms I'm cooking with.

When it comes to true wild mushrooms—the luscious chanterelles, morels, porcini, chicken of the woods, lobster mushrooms, and the like—you're starting to get something different, but the cost can be prohibitive. At over $20 a pound, I consider their purchase quite a luxury. Fortunately, I'm able to find my own wild mushrooms, and I always look for them at farmers' markets. If the cost is prohibitive, buy what you can afford and mix them with the common market mushrooms, in hope that the flavor and great looks of these unusual fungi will take over.

Oils

Mostly I cook with extra virgin olive oil. All different grades are available, some more expensive than others. I save my best oils for finishing a dish and cook with the less expensive olive oils.

On those rare occasions when I don't want the flavor of olive oil, I turn to an organic French sunflower seed oil that I've found at good-quality supermarkets. Although neutral, it's not without warmth, and I far prefer it to canola and generic vegetable oils. When I want an oil that is really neutral, I use a light peanut oil. I find safflower and soy are too often off-tasting, hinting of rancidity. Dark sesame and roasted peanut oils are terrific in tofu dishes.

Salt Capers

Dry and crusted with salt, they need to be rinsed, then soaked in water or in a few changes of water for 15 minutes or so, to rid them of excess salt. Once soaked, they open up into little flowers and have a lovely perfumed flavor, quite unlike capers that come packed in brine.

Note: Page numbers in **bold** indicate photographs.